Trafalgar Geordies
and North Country Seamen of Nelson's Navy 1793-1815

Tony Barrow

north east
england

© Tony Barrow

ISBN 1 905438 00 1

First published 2005

Cover Design by Tim Murphy Creative Solutions

With thanks to Tyne & Wear Museums and Sea Britain 2005 for endorsing this publication.

Published in Great Britain by
North East England Press
The Teleport
Doxford International
Sunderland
SR3 3XD

Tel: 0191 5252410
Fax: 0191 5201815

British Cataloguing-in-Publications Data
A catalogue record for this book is available from the British Library

Printed in Great Britain by the Alden Group, Oxford.

For my daughters
Harriet, Ailsa, Amy and Emma

Contents

Illustrations

Cover

The 'Defence' at the Battle of the First of June, 1794
National Maritime Museum, London

Part One Inserts

Part Two Inserts

Preface

This year the public of North East England will have the opportunity to participate in a range of activities associated with the commemoration of two notable events in British history; the sixtieth anniversary of the end of the Second World War and the bicentenary of the battle of Trafalgar. The artefacts and displays associated with a travelling exhibition of the Imperial War Museum, to be staged at various places around the country during 2005, has given an emphasis to popular testimony and the experience of ordinary civilians in wartime. The Trafalgar bicentenary events will, no doubt, give an emphasis to Lord Nelson and his 'band of brothers' in celebrating the rich diversity of Britain's maritime heritage during this 'Year of the Sea'. When Tall Ships enter the Tyne in July and sail up the river to Newcastle, they pass two monuments that commemorate different aspects of North East England's contribution to that maritime heritage. The Collingwood Monument, on the north bank of the river at Tynemouth, is dedicated to the achievement of Vice-Admiral Lord Collingwood who led the British fleet into action at Trafalgar on 21 October 1805. The monument was completed in 1845 and also celebrates an anniversary in 2005. A second, less conspicuous but no less significant monument stands close to the Customs House on the south bank of the river at South Shields. It commemorates the sacrifice of thousands of local seamen who lost their lives on merchant ships during the Second World War. Some of those unfortunate men were descendants of keelmen, whalermen and collier seamen pressed into naval service between 1793 and 1815.

This short book offers an insight into the lives and experience of those local mariners who fought the ships of Nelson's navy. It is intended as a small contribution to the maritime celebrations of the 'Year of the Sea'. The content will be of interest to maritime historians and genealogists as well as those who take a general interest in the history of the region. As a native of North East England the author is well aware that his use of the term 'Geordie' might meet with disapproval in some parts of the region, particularly on Wearside. Modern-day, intra-regional usage attaches a more specific definition to the word than it did in the past. However, for those who live elsewhere 'Geordie' is a generic term, used more loosely, and applied broadly to the inhabitants of south Northumberland and north Durham. 'North Country' is an old phrase traditionally used to refer to the whole of Northumberland, Durham and the North Riding of Yorkshire.

Writing a book within the constraints of time and personal circumstances would be impossible without the active support and encouragement of family, friends and fellow professionals. Accordingly, it only remains for me to thank all those who have given of their time, knowledge and expertise during the research and writing stages. In particular, Professor Norman McCord whose published work about press gangs and aspects of the labour history of merchant seamen in North East England continues to provide the foundation and insight necessary to any new research into the maritime history of the region. Professor McCord's observations and constructive suggestions relating to preliminary, draft chapters of the book have undoubtedly improved the content and quality of the final product. Regular access to the encyclopaedic knowledge of Adrian Osler, friend and fellow traveller in the waters of all things maritime, eased the burden of research and he will recognise his many contributions to the content of this book. Ian Whitehead, curator of maritime collections at Tyne Wear Museums, has been a constant source of encouragement and advice particularly in relation to identifying, and allowing access to, potential illustrative sources in the collections of regional museums and art galleries. Amongst numerous other people who have given generously of their time and resources special mention should be made of Vera Vaggs, local representative of The Nelson Society in Northumberland, for her hospitality in allowing me into her home to consult books and journals during the early stages of my research. Anthea Lang, local studies librarian at Gateshead Central Library made a particular contribution to this book by providing information about the names of seamen from North East England who served on *Leviathan* at Trafalgar. I take this opportunity to express my thanks for it. As always, colleagues and fellow historians Mike Furlonger and Dr. Liz O'Donnell have supported the venture from the outset, nor can I ignore the value of numerous conversations with Dr. David Ridley whose dedication to the task of recovering the labour history of the Durham pitmen has many similarities to my own research of the region's merchant seamen. Thanks are also due to Andrea Murphy, Sonya Miller and Moira Page of Business Education Publishers for the courtesy and care with which they have brought the manuscript to publication.

Last, but by no means least, the ongoing moral support and practical assistance of members of my family demands a mention in dispatches. Once again, Pat Barrow has brought her ICT skills and meticulous attention to detail to the proof-reading and standardisation of the typescript. Amy and Andy for their hospitality at St. Albans during research visits to the National Archives at Kew and the National Maritime Museum at Greenwich. Ailsa, Harriet and my wife Val can finally look forward to a measure of normality after tolerating long periods of silent reflection and facilitating the seclusion of my domestic exile during the months it has taken me to write this book.

Tony Barrow
Embleton,
Northumberland
April 2005

Biography

Tony Barrow is Lecturer in History and Archaeology at Newcastle College and an Associate Lecturer of the Open University. He studied at Newcastle University and obtained his Ph.D from the University of Northumbria in 1989, for research into The North East Coast Whaling Trade 1750-1850. He is widely consulted for his knowledge of regional ships and shipping in the age of sail, and is the author of numerous books and articles about the maritime history of the region. His other books include; *Tall Ships: Two Rivers* (with A. Osler); *Press Gangs and Privateers: Aspects of the Maritime History of North East England; Walks around the Old Coal Ports of Northumberland* and its companion volume *Walks around the Old Grain Ports of Northumberland; The Whaling Trade of North-East England 1750-1850; Britain and the Baltic Studies in Commercial, Political and Cultural Relations 1500-2000* (Edited with P. Salmon).

Introduction

At the end of the eighteenth century the maritime communities of North East England contained one of the most important concentrations of skilled mariners anywhere in the United Kingdom. Taken together, Newcastle and Sunderland were second only to London in the number of seamen they were obliged to provide for naval service under the terms of Pitt's Quota Acts of 1795. As a region, North East England provided almost three thousand men per annum under the Quota scheme. In an age when Britain trusted her security and defence to the navy, these local mariners became prime targets of the press gang and, as a result, many spent at least some of their careers manning the wooden walls of the Georgian navy. From Berwick in the north to Whitby and Scarborough in the south, thousands of seamen from the region fought and died on warships during the numerous wars of the eighteenth and early nineteenth centuries. Their names and personal details can be found in the muster books of British warships but in the majority of cases their lives and careers remain a mystery to us. Occasionally the records allow more detailed biographies to be constructed, usually when local seamen became involved in memorable maritime events. Men like Jack Crawford of Sunderland, a keelman, whose exploits aboard *Venerable* at the battle of Camperdown in 1797 made him a national hero and gained him a pension for life for services to his country. By contrast the career of Thomas McIntosh, who came from North Shields, is hardly known despite the biographical detail that survives about him. McIntosh was twenty-eight years old and rated carpenter's mate in the crew of *Bounty* during the notorious mutiny of 1789. Fletcher Christian forced him to remain on board because he needed his skills to maintain the ship even though McIntosh was a loyalist and took no part in the mutiny. He called out to Bligh to remember his loyalty when the captain was cast adrift in an open boat. McIntosh remained in Tahiti and was arrested when Bligh returned to find the mutineers. He survived the wreck of *Pandora* on the Great Barrier Reef and was acquitted at a court martial. Nothing is known about his subsequent career.[1]

Local seamen such as McIntosh and Crawford served their country with distinction in all the major naval battles of the Napoleonic era; Glorious First of June 1794, Camperdown and Cape St. Vincent 1797, the Nile 1798 and Copenhagen 1801. The triumph of their achievement and the best-known in popular imagination was the battle of Trafalgar fought on 21 October 1805. Men from North East England, over five hundred in total, were represented amongst the crew of every ship of the line that went into action that day. There were over fifty on *Colossus* and thirty or more on *Victory, Prince* and *Revenge*. It was hardly surprising therefore, that when the casualties were counted over seventy had been killed, wounded or drowned. Some of those fortunate enough to survive Trafalgar lost their lives in one of the many subsequent engagements of the war and only a minority lived long enough to claim their Trafalgar medal in 1848.

As Britain celebrates the bicentenary of the Battle of Trafalgar and the achievements of "the immortal Nelson" and "that noble fellow, Collingwood", it is easy to overlook the contribution of thousands of common seamen who fought the guns of the British fleet that day. Without them victory at Trafalgar could not have been achieved. *Trafalgar Geordies and North Country Seamen* is an attempt to recover the contribution of those 'ordinary' men.

References

1. Pitcairn Islands Study Centre @ http://library.puc.edu/pitcairn/bounty/crew3.shtml#mcintosh

'I shall have the great pleasure in doing every kindness in my power for a young man for whom Mr. Blackett has expressed himself so much interested. I hope he will live and prosper in the service to your utmost wish.'

[Admiral Collingwood to Samuel Castle,
26 September 1803]

The Royal Navy and the French Wars

When France declared war against Great Britain on 1 February 1793 it began a conflict that lasted more than twenty years. French armies dominated Europe for much of that time as the great powers struggled to cope with the genius of Napoleon. It was a different story at sea where the French Wars represented the end game of a series of conflicts that had their origins in the reign of Louis XIV more than a century before. Britain and France were imperial powers and their long quest for dominance was played out on a world stage in India, North America and the West Indies. Naval supremacy in the Gulf of St. Lawrence secured Wolfe's victory in Canada in 1759. Alternatively, French intervention and British naval weakness were decisive in provoking the surrender of Cornwallis at Yorktown in 1781 and instrumental in the subsequent loss of the American colonies in 1783. The American War of Independence strained British resources almost to breaking point. Nevertheless, in naval terms at least, a ten-year interlude before the outbreak of the French Revolutionary War proved to be more beneficial to the British than it did to the French.

The strategic role of the Royal Navy during wartime was essentially defensive; to prevent invasion and protect British trade. In military terms Britain never seriously considered a full-scale invasion of France preferring instead to subsidise the armies of friendly continental powers or occasionally indulge in amphibious operations. By contrast, France contemplated an invasion of Great Britain on several occasions. The most potent threat came between 1803 and 1805 when Napoleon ordered the construction of hundreds of shallow draught boats in the ports of northern France to transport his troops and equipment across to England. For such a plan to be successful, Napoleon knew that the French fleet needed to gain a temporary superiority in the English Channel, but this was easier said than done. Nevertheless, the constant presence of a large French Atlantic fleet at Brest and other ports in Brittany, less than two days sail from the English coast in favourable conditions, represented a constant threat. France also threatened British interests in the Mediterranean from her naval base at Toulon and to make matters worse, periodic alliances between France and Spain brought a potentially powerful Spanish fleet into play.

As a counter to these threats the Admiralty maintained two large fleets in European waters; the Channel Fleet based at Portsmouth and Plymouth and the Mediterranean Fleet which had no permanent base but was able to use Lisbon, a safe anchorage at Gibraltar and, before 1802, Port Mahon in Minorca for repair and supplies. Smaller fleets were maintained on the West Indies station and elsewhere throughout the war but the protection of home waters was always given priority. The Channel Fleet comprised twenty-six ships of the line in 1795 and there were thirty-five ships of the line and sixteen frigates at the time of Trafalgar in 1805.[1] These warships were principally used to blockade the French fleet in their home ports and prevent them from putting to sea. This could be done in a number of ways. At the beginning of the French Revolutionary War in 1793 Admiral Lord Howe implemented a policy of 'open blockade' by stationing some of his frigates off Brest so that they could report any French moves to prepare their vessels for sea. It enabled Howe's main force to remain at anchor until any real threat developed but offered opportunities for the French fleet to break out, which it did several times, and it was generally thought to be poor for morale. 'Close blockade' which was more commonly used after 1797 involved keeping a sufficient number of ships of the line constantly at sea so that they could respond more rapidly to a developing situation. Such tactics represented a double-edged sword. On the one hand it contributed substantially to the discipline, skills and experience of British seamen compared to their French counterparts. On the other hand it increased the risk of damage to ships from stress of weather and general wear and tear. 'Close blockade' could also be monotonous as well as dangerous. Collingwood summed up his own experience in a letter to his father-in-law Erasmus Blackett:

Barfleur off Brest,
4 July 1801

I have constantly been at sea except a fortnight, and in the present state of things have no expectation of coming in until the October gales drives us for shelter from them. Nothing can be duller than this sort of cruising to watch a port – the ships dawdling after one another for months together every day the same object in sight and that not a beautiful one but the bleak and barren rocks of Ushant.[2]

Ironically, many of the British warships so hastily commissioned for service in the Channel Fleet during the winter of 1792-93 were influenced by French designs. French warships, but particularly frigates and ships of the line, reached the peak of their reputation during the American War and the Admiralty took a keen interest in their construction and design. The development of the 74-gun ship of the line was influenced by the French *Invincible* captured in 1747 whereas *Courageux,* captured in 1761, was directly copied for four ships of the *Leviathan* class, some of which fought at Trafalgar in 1805.[3] In addition, numerous French warships captured by the British during the early years of the war, such as *Belleisle* [74], taken off Lorient in 1795, and *Tonnant* [80],* captured at the Battle of the Nile in 1798, also found their way into the British fleet that fought at Trafalgar.

At the outbreak of the French War the Royal Navy had fewer than five hundred vessels available for service. However, less than a third were in commission and only twenty-six of them were ships of the line. Most of the remainder were laid up 'in ordinary', maintained but neither rigged nor manned.[4] In January-February 1793 the Admiralty began the process of bringing some of these ships into commission; *Royal Sovereign* [100], was amongst the earliest to be brought into a state of readiness at Plymouth; *Agamemnon* [64], and *Bellerophon* [74], were both commissioned at Chatham during February-March 1793. Others quickly followed and the completion of warships already on the stocks, such as *Minotaur* [74], another ship destined to fight at Trafalgar, was speeded up.

Although there were numerous 98 and 100-gun ships in service with the British fleet throughout the French Wars, about half of all ships of the line in the Royal Navy in 1793 carried seventy-four guns like *Bellerophon* and *Minotaur.* They came to represent an ideal compromise between heavy armament and superior sailing qualities and were the type of warship with which British seamen were most familiar in the Age of Nelson. The so-called 'Common Class' of seventy-fours were two-deck vessels built to the designs of Sir Thomas Slade, formerly Surveyor to the Navy Board and arguably the most successful warship designer of the age of sail.

---

* The numbers in [ ] square brackets behind a ship's name denotes the number of guns it carried.

Bellerophon, for example, was typical of the class at 168 feet long, almost 50 feet wide and displacing 1604 tons. She carried 28x32 pound cannon on the main gun deck, 28x18 pound cannon on the upper deck and 18x9 pound guns on the forecastle and quarterdeck. *Bellerophon* also carried carronades and other guns in addition to her main armament.[5] Warships like this cost almost £44,000 to build in 1789 and perhaps £50,000 or more during the Napoleonic War. In addition, the costs associated with providing the logistical support necessary to sustain several fleets of such vessels simultaneously, at sea, or refitting in one of the King's dockyards represented an enormous commitment in manpower and resources. In 1793 Parliament voted four million pounds for the service of the navy. By 1797 this figure had doubled and it rose further to fourteen million pounds by 1801. The bulk of the money, almost 86 per cent in 1801, went to the cost of paying the wages of officers and men.[6] A 74-gun ship probably cost, at a conservative estimate, between £800-£850 per month in wages alone during the 1790s and well over £1000 per month to keep at sea. Little wonder that the Prime Minister, William Pitt, developed a reputation as the most ingenious tax-gatherer ever to govern England. His many schemes for raising revenue included the introduction of income tax in 1797.

The naval officers appointed to command these ships were a professional elite whose training and continuity of service represented one of the principal strengths of the Georgian navy. When war was declared, many of them were semi-retired, on half-pay but ready to resume their active careers at sea. They included, of course, a number of naval officers from North East England. The best known was Cuthbert Collingwood (1748-1810) who entered the navy as an thirteen year old in 1761. Collingwood's distinguished career was sponsored by his uncle, Captain (later Admiral) Braithwaite, nurtured by Robert Roddam, another Northumbrian admiral, who was then captain of *Lennox* [74] at Portsmouth, and consolidated by his own experience as a lieutenant on the American and West Indies stations during the War of Independence. Collingwood was promoted lieutenant on the same day he was engaged supplying troops at the battle of Bunker Hill in 1775. He became a post-captain in 1781. It was during his service in America that Collingwood first met and struck up a lasting friendship with Horatio Nelson.

At the outbreak of the French War in 1793 Collingwood was appointed flag-captain to Rear-Admiral Sir George Bowyer, another old friend, and placed in command of *Prince* [98]. It was the largest vessel Collingwood had commanded to that date although he was unimpressed by her sailing qualities '…the most miserable sailer in the fleet and forever in the rear'.[7] He subsequently transferred with Bowyer into the older but faster *Barfleur* [98] in time for the first major naval engagement of the war; the battle of the Glorious First of June in 1794. Another naval officer from Newcastle who fought at that battle was Edward Rotheram (1753-1830) who was destined to become Collingwood's flag-captain at Trafalgar. He was born in Hexham, the son of a medical doctor who later moved to Newcastle to practice. Rotheram first learnt his skills in the coal trade and joined the Royal Navy relatively late, at the age of twenty-three, in 1777. He was promoted quickly and served as an acting-lieutenant of *Monarch* in the West Indies where his ship took part in several fleet actions. As first lieutenant of *Culloden* [74] in 1793, Rotheram distinguished himself during the battle of the Glorious First of June and was promoted commander soon afterwards.[8] Other naval officers from North East England destined to play a famous role at Trafalgar included Robert Moorsom (1760-1835), son of a Whitby whaler owner and captain of *Revenge* [74] and William Pryce Cumby (1771-1837) of Heighington, near Darlington. Moorsom like Rotheram entered the navy in 1777. He became a captain in 1790 and commanded frigates during the early years of the French Revolutionary War. Cumby was the son of a naval captain and entered the navy at the age of eight! He was appointed lieutenant of *Assistance* [50] in October 1793 then part of the Channel Fleet. The captain of *Assistance* was Nathan Brunton, a family friend from Stockton-on-Tees and another naval officer from the region.[9]

Family connections and professional followings were vital to the promotion prospects and careers of eighteenth century naval officers like Cumby and Collingwood. In their turn both men sought to facilitate the entry and advancement of young men recommended to them. Collingwood in particular took a personal interest in young officers from his native Northumberland and his correspondence is full of references to them.

When he moved from *Hector* to *Excellent* in 1795, Collingwood took a number of midshipmen with him, five of them were from Newcastle. George Fogo, then aged twenty-two, joined Collingwood in April 1793. He was wounded at the battle of the Glorious First of June and also fought at the battle of Cape St. Vincent in 1797. Another Newcastle-born midshipman, Jonathan Bell, was promoted Master's Mate soon after he joined Collingwood on *Excellent*.[10] Of course, some of these young men from Newcastle failed to live up to the recommendation of their sponsors. Collingwood wrote from *Excellent* at Portsmouth in July 1795:

> I had three Richardsons here the other day but shall only carry one to sea…the eldest was not a person by any means entitled and if I had known the state he was in before he came here I would not have received such an expense and burden on the service… if he should have come from any other quarter I should have sent his enrolment to the Admiralty…but the rest behave very well.[11]

Only the youngest of the Richardson brothers appears to have satisfied Collingwood's rigorous standards. Henry Richardson was promoted midshipman in July 1795 and was second lieutenant of *Excellent* at the battle of Cape St. Vincent in February 1797.[12] Another young officer of *Excellent* was William Christie (1771-1858) who came from Boldon in County Durham where Erasmus Blackett's brother was Rector. Christie entered the navy as an able seaman but was rated as a schoolmaster in February 1795. He taught mathematics and principles of navigation to the midshipmen. Collingwood obviously had a good opinion of him and sought to further promote his naval career:

> I shall give Christie what money may be necessary for him, but I wished to see a little more of him first – what I have seen I like very well and if the war continues I will bring him forward into the best situation that I can...[13]

Christie's short, personal account of his experience at the battle of Cape St. Vincent in 1797 is contained in a letter to his patron, Erasmus Blackett and offers an interesting insight into the realities of a naval encounter of that period. Christie wrote:

> In the action I noted signals and made remarks, an unpleasant situation I assure you, it is not easy in the heat of battle to write with composure. I will fairly tell you I could not have solved a problem in the mathematics![14]

Christie was subsequently promoted purser on Collingwood's recommendation and went on to serve in that capacity on various warships throughout the French Wars. It was a responsible and potentially lucrative position, much sought after but by no means easy to obtain. Pursers were, in effect, the ship's accountant and stores manager and as such were required to handle considerable sums of money. It was the practice, therefore, upon first appointment that pursers paid a surety of between £400-£1000 depending upon the rate of the ship, as a guarantee of their trustworthiness and suitability for the post. As his patron, Blackett stood guarantor for Christie who had been appointed purser of the frigate *L'Unite* [38], captured by a squadron under Sir Edward Pellew off the French coast the year before. Blackett is likely to have paid about £500 to facilitate the development of his career as a warrant officer in the Royal Navy. Christie acknowledged his gratitude to Blackett in a letter from Plymouth in March 1798:

> *L'Unite,* Plymouth Dock,
> 12 March 1798

> I thank you for the kind step you have taken in my favour and hope that my frugality and attention to business will soon put it in my power to replace the sum that you have been pleased to give me credit for...we expect to sail today or the next day when we hope to be more fortunate than in our last cruize [sic].[15]

Appointment to a frigate gave Christie good prospects of prize money and the means of settling his debt to Blackett within a few years. Pursers had a poor reputation amongst seamen in the Royal Navy because they were suspected, with some justification, of embezzling ship's stores, giving short weight and exploiting the needs of seamen. It was said for example that a purser's pound amounted to fourteen ounces rather than sixteen and that he supplied the men tobacco and 'slops' at exorbitant rates. These were criticisms of the post rather than the individual who filled it but the records suggest that some pursers were clearly rapacious and justified the suspicions of the seamen they exploited. Whether William Christie was a 'good' or a 'bad' purser is lost to the historical record but he served on various ships throughout the French and Napoleonic Wars. He ended his naval service as purser of *Northumberland* [74] the vessel designated to carry Napoleon into his final exile on St. Helena in 1815.

After several further changes of ship, Collingwood returned to *Barfleur* in 1801 and remained in command of her until the cessation of hostilities the following year. From time to time he continued to express his concerns about the attitude and character of some of the prospective young men from North East England who had been recommended to him:

> Has he been taught navigation?…boys make very little progress in a ship without being well practiced in navigation; and fifteen is too old to begin… He will never come on deck but when he is sent for by some officer and does nothing below. And yet he messes with some of the finest boys that are in the Navy. The Newcastle boys do not prosper, at least in my hands.[16]

Many of them did, of course, and Collingwood was especially pleased with the volunteers he received into *Venerable* in September 1803:

> …the Newcastle volunteers, with the two youngsters joined about a fortnight since, they are a set of stout young men and a great addition to my strength, my ship now being very well manned…[17]

The two 'youngsters' to which Collingwood's letter referred were both destined to fight at the battle of Trafalgar. Grenville Thompson was fifteen years old and the son of a Newcastle merchant with premises in The Side. The other was George Castle then aged fourteen, the son of a Durham solicitor and a business associate of Blackett. The exchange of correspondence between Collingwood, Blackett and Castle offers an interesting insight into the process of patronage and influence so common in the society of that age. In August 1803 Samuel Castle, the young man's father, wrote to Blackett:

I trouble you with this again to repeat my thanks and to mention how very pleasant it is that my wife and son can do the business at Portsmouth…my wife and son will set out on Monday morning, they cannot sooner…your good wishes must prevail and I have no fears…

About three weeks later on 18 September, Samuel Castle wrote again to Blackett:

Dear Sir,

Expecting my wife home today…I am able to say that she arrived safe in the mail this morning after performing the journey and managing the business very satisfactorily. She saw my son on board the *Puissant* receiving ship last Monday to go from thence into the *Magnificent,* Captain James, to Admiral Collingwood in the Channel Fleet.

After they had relieved themselves by a few tears in private, the lad in a most manly way, requested his mother not to go to the waterside with him – he did not wish either to heighten her distress or his own, or be seen whimpering…thus is launched into the busy world (I have the comfort to hope) another hero for further glory in future to his country, and heaven will bless the kind exertions you have bestowed upon him…[18]

May God be with the *Venerable* as he was at Camperdown

Samuel Castle

The boys reached Collingwood's flagship patrolling off Brest a week later and the Admiral wrote in polite and reassuring terms to Castle's anxious parents:

Venerable, off Brest
26 September 1803

Sir,

I have the pleasure to acquaint you that your son arrived on board this ship yesterday in good health and spirits; by him I received the favour of your letter. I shall have the great pleasure in doing every kindness in my power for a young man for whom Mr. Blackett has expressed himself so much interested. I was on this account prepared to give him a kind reception but independent of so favourable an introduction, his manners and appearance at first sight would have obtained for him regard. He seems a sprightly, spirited youth and there is no doubt will in due time make a good officer. It would have been a great advantage to him to have got a little more mathematics before he embarked but as it is he must make the best of the opportunities that offer.

I shall take care that whatever is necessary for him shall be provided – which I expect will be no great expense – for in proportion as he applies himself to his duty, his expenses will be less – I hope he will live and prosper in the service to your utmost wish.[19]

As young midshipmen, George Castle and Grenville Thompson followed Collingwood from ship to ship between 1803 and 1805. They transferred with Vice-Admiral Collingwood, Captain Rotheram and others from *Dreadnought* into *Royal Sovereign* on 11 October 1805 a week before Trafalgar. Thompson was badly wounded in the battle and Castle was destined to write one of the few eyewitness accounts of the action from the perspective of a young, Durham-born officer.

References

1. Lavery, B. *Nelson's Navy: The Ships, Men and Organisation 1793-1815,* Conway Maritime Press (London, 1989), p. 245.

2. Admiral Collingwood to Erasmus Blackett, 4 July 1801, Northumberland Record Office (NRO), ZBL 247.

3. Lavery, *Nelson's Navy,* p. 47.

4. Northcote-Parkinson, C. *Britannia Rules: The Classic Age of Naval History 1793-1815,* Alan Sutton Publishing Ltd. (Stroud, 1994), p. 9.

5. Cordingly, D. *Billy Ruffian: The Bellerophon and the Downfall of Napoleon. The biography of a ship of the line,* Bloomsbury Publishing PLC (London, 2003), pp. 12-13.

6. The figures are based on the naval estimates cited in Lavery, *Nelson's Navy,* p. 21.

7. Klukvin, B. *Vice-Admiral Lord Collingwood,* Oriel Press (Newcastle, 1972), p. 10.

8. National Archives (NA), ADM 9/2/142.

9. Jackson, H.W. *A County Durham Man at Trafalgar: Cumby of the Bellerophon,* Durham County Local History Society (Durham, 1997).

10. Muster Book of *Excellent,* NA, ADM 36/11880.

11. Admiral Collingwood to Erasmus Blackett, 8 July 1795, NRO, ZBL 247.

12. Muster Book of *Excellent*, NA, ADM 36/11880.

13. Admiral Collingwood to Erasmus Blackett, 7 November 1794, NRO, ZBL 247.

14. William Christie to Erasmus Blackett, 18 February 1797, *Letters from Cuthbert Collingwood to Dr. Carlyle of Inveresk and Mrs. Carlyle*, Newcastle Central Library (NCL), Letter 40. Carlyle married Mary Roddam who with her sister Sarah was adopted and brought up by Admiral Roddam and his wife.

15. William Christie to Erasmus Blackett, 12 March 1798, NRO, ZBL 228.

16. Klukvin, *Collingwood*, p. 18.

17. Admiral Collingwood to Erasmus Blackett, 10 October 1803, *Letters from Collingwood to Dr. Carlyle*, NCL, Letter 31.

18. Samuel Castle to Erasmus Blackett, 29 August and 18 September 1803, NRO, ZBL 228.

19. Admiral Collingwood to Samuel Castle, 26 September 1803, NRO, ZBL 247.

'...the seamen in this ship are sour and any little matter would make a convulsion right now...'

[Admiral Collingwood to Erasmus Blackett, 3 August 1794]

Naval Recruitment and Conditions of Service

Notwithstanding the hazards of battle and the dangers of the sea, the career prospects of a commissioned officer in Nelson's navy were generally good and there was never a shortage of applicants from the younger sons of the gentry or, like Castle and Thompson, from the mercantile and professional classes. By contrast, the recruitment of seamen was more problematic. Skilled craftsmen like carpenters or experienced seamen who rose to become boatswains and gunners, could always find security of employment as warrant officers because they remained with their ships even when they were laid up, out of commission. These warrant officers often came to be associated with the sea-going careers of particular naval officers and some even rose to become officers themselves or were able to use what influence they had to promote the careers of their own children. The son of Alexander Galloway, for example, a naval boatswain from Guisborough, was a fourteen-year old midshipman of *Thunderer* [74] at Trafalgar.[1]

During the mid-eighteenth century it was common for naval officers to recruit seamen from the county or town of their birth. With its long coastline, numerous ports and thriving maritime communities, North East England was the home of a number of naval captains who looked to recruit men from the region. Robert Roddam, for example, attracted numerous volunteers from North East England during his long career as a naval officer. Volunteers from Newcastle and Northumberland served under him on *Greenwich* in the West Indies during the Seven Years War and continued to do so later in his career. In January 1771, for example, soon after Roddam had been appointed to command *Lennox* at Portsmouth, the muster book recorded the names of fifteen seamen from North East England all of whom were entered as volunteers. The majority came from Newcastle and Shields and their consecutive muster numbers, together with the fact that over half of them were initially rated as Ordinary Seamen, suggests that they had arrived together in a batch.[2] Amongst the young officers commanding them were the Collingwood brothers, Cuthbert and Wilfred, who served together as young midshipmen of *Lennox*. Collingwood was another naval officer conspicuous in his efforts to preserve the tradition of recruiting seamen from North East England into his ships '...being particularly connected with Newcastle, I engaged my friends there to use their influence with the seamen, which they did so effectively that fifty men entered'.[3]

As late as September 1803 when Collingwood received the two youngsters Castle and Thompson into *Venerable,* over two hundred volunteers from North East England accompanied them although this was probably exceptional. Many of these volunteers were destined to fight at Trafalgar.

Collingwood, like the Admiralty, was well aware of the quality of local seamen. The majority learnt their skills in the collier brigs of Shields, Sunderland, Blyth or Whitby. The coal trade was not only economically vital to the country, it was one of the principal sources of experienced mariners and had been recognised as such for generations. As early as 1615 it was observed that 'The Newcastle Voyage, if not the only, yet is the especial nursery and school of seamen, so is it the gentlest and most open to landsmen'.[4]

Colliers were generally larger than the vessels usually engaged in the coasting trades and it was common for seamen to sail them all year round. By the end of the eighteenth century most large colliers were making six to eight round voyages per year. The hardships and hazards associated with navigating deeply laden colliers through the shoals and sandbanks of the east coast of Britain, in all weathers, created a special breed of seamen. In order to maintain a steady supply of new recruits, the coal trade was heavily regulated by government, particularly in respect of the number of apprentices colliers were obliged to carry. Boys between the ages of ten and thirteen were usually apprenticed for between three and seven years, depending upon their social background. Pauper apprentices, for example, could be apprenticed for up to nine years and were not entitled to receive wages during this time. These were probably the conditions imposed upon young William Allen of North Shields, recorded on the muster roll of *Northumberland* in December 1778 as an apprentice 'from the poore house'. Colliers appear to have carried one apprentice for every fifty tons of their burden, although the actual number varied in peace and war. In 1769 *Wellington* of Newcastle, 200 tons, regularly carried four apprentices, whereas *Albion* of Shields, also 200 tons, carried three, two fourteen-year olds and a boy of fifteen.[5] Some of these young men went on to command their own vessels in the coal trade and passed on their skills to the generation of seamen that manned Nelson's navy. Men like Thomas Scain who served a seven-year apprenticeship on *Aurora*, James Barrass who served a six-year apprenticeship on the brig *Riga Merchant* and William Sim who served for four years as an apprentice on *Amphitrite,* one of the best known of the old Shields collier brigs. As young men just out of their apprenticeships they were all subsequently impressed into the navy after 1793. Scain fought on the middle gun deck of *Queen* [98] at the battle of the Glorious First of June in 1794 while Sim was wounded on board *Orion* [74] at Trafalgar.[6]

The experience of Scain, Barrass and Sim was typical of hundreds of merchant seamen from North East England at the end of the eighteenth century. But collier seamen also developed a broader experience of voyages across the North Sea and into the Baltic. Typically, a Newcastle or Whitby collier might undertake a coal voyage to London, then sail out to the Baltic from the Thames in ballast and return to an east coast port with timber, tar, iron or hemp. During 1784-85, for example, *Forrester* of Shields undertook several repeat voyages in the coal trade, brought 1600 barrels of tar from Archangel, delivered a cargo of Baltic timber at King's Lynn and then sailed from Shields to Marseilles with coal. The largest vessels at Whitby and Newcastle even combined seasonal voyages to the Greenland Whale Fishery with coal and Baltic voyages later in the year. The participation of local vessels in whaling activity had considerable economic and commercial importance for the region. It also facilitated the development of whaling skills amongst local seamen and created a distinct category of mariners who were known to their nautical contemporaries as 'Greenlanders'.

Like the coal trade, the 'Greenland Fishery' was considered a nursery of seamen and subject to strict regulation. Since the establishment of a home-grown whaling industry was entirely dependent upon the development of whaling skills amongst British seamen, 'Greenlanders' enjoyed certain rights and privileges including certificates of protection from impressment. Harpooners, boatsteerers and linemanagers were entitled to year-round protection which included their voyages in the coal trade during the winter months. Other seamen, learning the skills of whaling, were given a protection certificate only for the duration of the voyage.[7] The depth and variety of experience associated with the working lives of these seamen at the end of the eighteenth century goes some way to explaining the early development of trade unionism and benevolent societies.

In explaining the development of trade unionism amongst the collier seamen, McCord was probably right to emphasise the importance of the short-haul, coasting voyages of the coal trade in multiplying the opportunities for contact and cohesion '…more than an emphasis on deep-sea voyages would have done'.[8] At the same time many collier seamen, such as those engaged in the whaling trade, regularly undertook long ocean voyages and the totality of their experience facilitated the development of a well-organised fraternity of seamen. In these circumstances it is hardly surprising that merchant seamen from North East England were amongst the earliest occupational groups to organise in defence of their common interests and strikes became an important part of the labour history of the coal trade. Trade disputes were usually associated with seamen's wages and conditions but also included their opposition to the activities of the press gang. Strikes, such as those of 1769, 1775 and 1787, effectively stopped any voyages in the coal trade for several weeks until the seamen's grievances were settled. In 1792, within a context of rising prices, the collier seamen demanded an increase of wages to £3 for a round voyage during the winter months and once again came out on strike. They enforced their demands by stopping the coal trade and removing crews from all of the ships then lying in the river Tyne. Seamen in colliers returning to the river quickly became involved as well and the strike soon became general as it spread to Sunderland and smaller coal ports like Blyth and Seaton Sluice. The success of the 1792 strike was due to the solidarity of the sailors and their willingness to accept the discipline of their elected representatives.[9]

In February 1793 as Britain entered the great wars with Revolutionary France, the same committee of collier seamen associated with the 1792 strike organised resistance to the activities of press gangs then operating at all of the principal ports of the region. This time the merchant seamen agitated for an improvement of pay and conditions in the Royal Navy.

Although more recent scholarship has gone some way towards ameliorating our image of naval conditions in Nelson's ships, it is clear that naval service remained unpopular for a number of reasons.[10] In a broadsheet published in Newcastle in February 1793 the merchant seamen skilfully articulated their principal concerns:

> If we are such friends to our countrymen that we are always ready to step forward in their defence, why should our situation in time of war be so much worse than in time of peace?[11]

The seamen's grievances centred on low pay, lack of facilities and inadequate provision to remit wages to their dependant relatives. In 1793 able seamen in the Royal Navy were paid twenty-two shillings (£1.10p) per month, a sum that had remained unchanged since Cromwell's time. It was significantly less than they could earn in almost any branch of the merchant service and to make matters worse the food was poor, the lower deck overcrowded and the discipline harsh. The absence of any system for registration of seamen and the practice of commissioning more warships when hostilities threatened, obliged the Admiralty to resort to press gangs to solve its chronic manning problem. In the first year of the French War the number of men serving in the Royal Navy increased more than five-fold, from 16,613 in 1792 to 87,331 in 1794. Hundreds of collier seamen from North East England were swept into naval service during these years and they took their organisation and grievances with them.

The Admiralty ignored their criticisms and the seamen's resentment grew. Collingwood was perceptive enough to read the warning signs. He alluded to the truculence of the seamen he encountered as well as cases of actual mutiny in several letters to his father-in-law, Erasmus Blackett. Soon after his appointment to *Hector* at Portsmouth in August 1794, Collingwood wrote:

> ...the seamen in this ship are sour, any little matter would make a convulsion right now. I have heard the *Barfleur's* have also shown symptoms of a dangerous restlessness when part of them was drafted into another ship...but the temperate and good management of Captain Elphinstone settled the business quietly...[but] I fear the seeds are sown. Let them take care the growth is checked dexterously or we will need no foreign enemy to confound us.[12]

Later, in November 1794 Collingwood again expressed his anxiety about the resentful attitude of seamen in the Channel Fleet:

> Affairs seem to be sadly out of joint – even our dependence on the navy seems by a late event to be very much weakened – from what circumstances it arose I do not know but I have heard by too rigorous a discipline in some young officers the ships company of the *Queen* revolted against their officers – threw off their obedience at sea and were absolutely in a state of mutiny.[13]

Some politicians were quick to blame the influence of radicals and revolutionary ideas for the seamen's discontent. Others, including Collingwood himself, blamed the impact of the so-called 'Quota Men' recruited into the Fleet as a result of the Quota Acts of 1795. Many were landsmen with few skills and no sea-going experience. Others were attracted by bounties offered by local authorities as an inducement to enlist. After 1795 these bounties were substantially higher than those paid to experienced seamen in 1793-94. At Stockton, for example, the local authorities issued a poster offering 'the largest bounties ever given' and were prepared to pay £31.5.0. to an able seaman willing to serve in the Fleet.[14] Such sums of money were deeply resented by experienced seamen pressed into service at the outbreak of the war. Collingwood believed that 'Billy Pitt's men':

> Embarked with their budget of politics and the education of a Sunday School into the ships where they disseminated their nonsense and mischief.[15]

Left-wing historians like E.P. Thompson attributed the origins and aims of the Great Mutinies to the agitation of political radicals or the activities of United Irishmen. In fact, the reasons for the seamen's discontent were more prosaic and pre-dated the Quota Acts; low pay, poor conditions and harsh discipline. In particular the excessive flogging of conscientious and experienced seamen that only served to further alienate men from their officers. After1793 there were fewer opportunities for naval officers like Collingwood to cultivate personal followings as the crews of large warships became more fluid and anonymous. The system of discipline developed to uphold the authority of a naval officer under these circumstances, even if, individually, they had done nothing to deserve the respect of their men, led to some notorious cases of brutality and eventually to mutinies.[16] Collingwood knew this very well. He condemned excessive flogging as '...big with the most dangerous consequences and subversive of all real discipline'.[17] Despite his own reputation as a firm disciplinarian, Collingwood was well known for the humane treatment of the seamen under his command and always endeavoured to accord them the respect he believed they deserved. Moreover, he insisted that his officers followed his example. In turn, seamen acknowledged Collingwood's skills and humanity as a naval officer:

A better seaman – a better friend to seamen – never trod a quarter-deck...a man who could not be happy under him, could have been happy nowhere; a look of displeasure from him was as bad as a dozen at the gangway from another man.[18]

The majority of naval officers appointed to command warships during the French Wars imposed their discipline sensibly. However, some naval captains developed unenviable reputations for abuse and tyrannical behaviour. George Irwin, a seaman from Hexham who volunteered at Shields in 1796, had the misfortune to be drafted to *Shannon* [32], Captain Fraser:

One of the most barbarous and one of the most unhuman (sic) officers that ever a sect of unfortunate men ever had the disagreeable misfortune of being with.[19]

Similar complaints of abuse and mistreatment were directed to the Admiralty in ever increasing numbers after 1795 and they form the backdrop to the outbreak of general mutiny in the Fleet in 1797.

The Great Mutinies began on the ships of the Channel Fleet at Spithead on Easter Monday 1797. The crews of sixteen ships of the line anchored in The Solent disobeyed orders to muster and refused to weigh anchor again until their grievances had been settled. The men elected delegates from each of the warships involved who met together as an organising committee on the flagship *Queen Charlotte* and negotiated the seamen's demands

with representatives of the Admiralty. They wanted an increase of
wages, allowance of provisions based upon sixteen ounces in the
pound rather than the purser's fourteen ounces, sufficient fresh
vegetables when they were in port, better treatment of sick and
wounded men and more opportunities for shore leave. When their
demands were finally conceded the delegates requested and
obtained a royal pardon from George III for all the men involved
in the mutiny. It was their insurance policy against a repetition of
the dishonesty and betrayal of the *Culloden* mutineers who had
been hanged in 1794 after promises of a pardon were ignored.[20]
The solidarity and discipline of the Spithead mutineers unsettled
the authorities and reflected the organisation and methods used
by the collier seamen during the strike of 1792. Despite the use of
informers and *agents provocateurs* the authorities were never able
to establish the names of the ringleaders. Valentine Joyce, delegate
of *Royal George* was thought to have been one of them; James
Melvin delegate of *La Pompee,* captured at the Glorious First of
June in 1794, was another, although neither admitted to being
so. Melvin, a thirty-four year old quartermaster from Sunderland,
was named in correspondence between Aaron Graham, a
magistrate sent down to Portsmouth by the Home Office to
investigate the cause of the mutiny. Graham hoped to detach Joyce
and Melvin from the other delegates and offered bribes for them
to turn informer:

> Hopes I have – and great ones too – of being able to
> secure the evidence of Joyce of the *Royal George* and
> Melvin of the *Pompee.* Graham found Joyce:
> …'obstinately silent', [but] with regard to Melvin I
> have the strongest assurances from a person who knows
> him intimately that he has more than once given hints
> that if he could be sure of his discharge from the service
> he should be glad to be taken from his present
> disagreeable situation. Such a promise I take for granted

I am authorised to make whenever it can be done for effect and as to pecuniary considerations they will not stand in my way.[21]

Graham's optimism was misplaced. Melvin was no more forthcoming than Joyce had been. The delegates maintained their solidarity and the authorities found it impossible to penetrate their organisation. Graham failed to discover any evidence that political radicals had incited the seamen to mutiny and was forced to conclude:

I am persuaded from the conversation I have had with so many of the sailors that nothing like want of loyalty to the king or attachment to the government can be traced in the business.[22]

Melvin was one of four seamen from North East England elected as delegates of the fleet during the Spithead mutiny. The others were, Thomas Allen an able seaman from Hartley in Northumberland, delegate of *Mars*, John Husband from Whitby, delegate of *Defiance* and John Scrivener from North Shields, delegate of *Robust*.[23]

In sharp contrast to the discipline and orderliness of the Spithead seamen, a second mutiny at the Nore in May-June 1797 was marked by disorder and violence and proved to be disastrously unsuccessful. Numerous seamen from North East England took part in the mutiny and some subsequently faced courts martial. The seamen at the Nore also elected delegates who met together as a strike committee on *Sandwich,* which became the focus of the mutiny. William Winship, an able seaman from Gateshead, and George Taylor a quartermaster from Sunderland, were both members of the committee. The muster books of *Sandwich, Monmouth, Inflexible* and several other ships involved in the mutiny indicate the names of numerous other men from the region whose records were endorsed 'a favourer of the mutiny' and who were subsequently disqualified.[24] Taylor in particular was lucky to escape with his life. The evidence given against him at his trial by several officers of *Sandwich* left little doubt that Taylor had played an active role in the mutiny:

> I considered him from the first day of the mutiny to the last as an active mutineer. He was frequently in armed boats and I have seen him going and coming from the Committee held on board the ship.[25]

Taylor forfeited his wages 'for mutiny and rebellion' and was sentenced to one-year's hard labour. Other ringleaders, including Richard Parker the acknowledged leader of the mutiny, were hanged from the yardarm. Twelve mutineers of *Inflexible,* three of them from North East England, escaped through the lower gun-ports, rowed their boats to Faversham, overpowered two boys guarding the sloop *Good Intent* and sailed it to Calais where they were arrested by the French authorities. The mutineers were released on condition that they agreed to serve on a French privateer![26]

Despite the failure of the Nore mutiny it is universally agreed that the year 1797 began a new era in the history of the Royal Navy and it is clear that the collier seamen of North East England contributed decisively to hard won improvements of pay and conditions on the lower deck. Local seamen involved in the Great Mutinies of 1797 went on to serve their country with distinction in the numerous naval engagements of the war. Thomas Allen, delegate of *Mars* at Spithead was subsequently promoted midshipman in June 1798, perhaps in recognition of the bravery he showed when *Mars* engaged *Hercule* in a bloody single-ship action off Brest earlier that year. The captain and twenty other officers and men were killed, thirty-seven were wounded. Allen remained in *Mars* until March 1800 when he was promoted lieutenant.[27] Many seamen associated with the mutiny at the Nore subsequently fought at the battle of Camperdown in October 1797 where Jack Crawford, a keelman from Sunderland on Admiral Duncan's flagship *Venerable*, was celebrated as a national hero. Less is known about numerous other local men who fought the guns of British ships engaged in that battle. Men like David Gray of South Shields, William Turner of North Shields, Jonathan Brown of Berwick and Richard Wrangham of Whitby, pressed from colliers into the crew of *Ardent* [64]. Under the command of Captain Richard Burgess, *Ardent* engaged the Dutch flagship *Vrijheid* but her crew suffered the bloody consequences of this privilege. Burgess was killed during the action together with forty members of his crew. Almost a hundred were wounded. The first lieutenant subsequently reported 'I am afraid that a great part of our wounded will die as they are in general dreadfully mangled…it is a wonder from the number of shot holes in her sides that we had not many more men killed.'[28]

Ardent with her masts and steering gear destroyed was towed back to England by *Bedford*. Having experienced the tumult of the Nore mutiny and the horrors of Camperdown able seamen David Gray, then aged twenty-two, ran from the ship at Chatham and returned to his native South Shields. Some time later he mustered to a Tyne whaler, probably *Middleton*, to learn the skills of the 'Greenlanders'. Gray moved with his family to Peterhead in 1810 where he began a famous career as a whaler captain.

At the battle of the Nile in August 1798, there were twelve seamen from North East England on Nelson's flagship *Vanguard*, including William Waller an able seaman from Stockton-on-Tees, aged twenty-two, who was killed during the battle.[29] Another seaman who fought at the battle was Peter Sadler, boatswain of *Orion,* who came from Cullercoats. He had been pressed into the navy from a fishing coble off the Tyne in 1793 and served ten years in the fleet before he was discharged.[30]

When the French Revolutionary War ended in March 1802 there were almost 129,000 men serving in the Royal Navy. Rapid demobilisation reduced this to less than 50,000 during the year following the Peace of Amiens but it proved to be a hasty and shortsighted decision. Napoleon's ambition could not be contained for long and hostilities were renewed in May 1803. Press warrants were issued, press gangs reformed and the Royal Navy brought back into a state of readiness. During the spring and summer of 1803 merchant seamen throughout the country suffered the consequences of a 'hot press' considered to have been one of the most ruthless and effective in the history of the press gang. George Irwin, the seaman from Hexham who had volunteered at Shields in 1796, had vivid memories of the event. He was one of the crew of the collier *Hercules* in-bound from Shields and anchored in the Thames near Woolwich:

> At night we set the watch and at twelve o'clock we were relieved. I went below to my hammock, when one of our men came down into the half deck; he says to me, 'Don't turn in yet, because there is something particular on the river tonight'. I asked him what made him think so; 'well', said he, 'I served my time to be a waterman on this river and by the plying of so many boats at this time of night, I am certain all cannot be well'. He no sooner had the word out of his mouth when two lusty marines rushed below, armed with each a cutlass and two pistols, without ceremony they took two of our men and left the ship. We then told the captain that our intention was to go ashore as it was evident that a press had broke out...[31]

Irwin evaded the gang on this occasion although it proved to be a temporary reprieve. He was pressed in London later the same year and drafted to *Polyphemus* [64] where he met twenty other seamen from North East England.

References

1. Muster book of *Thunderer*, NA, ADM 37/192-193 derived from the Ayshford Complete Trafalgar Roll.

2. Muster books of *Greenwich* (1755-56) and *Lennox* (1771-72), ADM 36/5673 and NA, ADM 36/7630.

3. Lavery, *Nelson's Navy*, p. 124.

4. Osler, A and Barrow, T. *Tall Ships: Two Rivers*, Keepdate (Newcastle 1992), p. 33.

5. Muster Rolls for the Port of Shields, NA, BT 98/124-129.

6. The Tyne Aged Sailors and Scullermen's Asylum, Annual Report 1843, Tyne Wear Archives Service (TWAS).

7. See, Barrow, T. *The Whaling Trade of North East England 1750-1850*, University of Sunderland Press, (Sunderland, 2001).

8. McCord, N. and Brewster, D.E. *Some Labour Troubles of the 1790s in North East England*, International Review of Social History, XIII (1968). p. 366.

9. Barrow, T. *The Greenlanders at Shields 1760-1830: A Labour Elite*, Bulletin of the North East Labour History Society, 24, (1990), p. 6.

10. Rodger, N.A.M. *The Wooden World.* Rodger, however, does concede that experienced seamen resented the harsh discipline and unreasonable shipboard practices of some officers. See note 16 (below).

11. Broadsheet addressed to Friends and Fellow Seaman, Newcastle, 2 February 1793, NCL.

12. Admiral Collingwood to Erasmus Blackett, 3 August 1794, *Letters from Captain Cuthbert Collingwood to Dr. Carlyle of Inveresk and Mrs. Carlyle*, NCL, Letter 5.

13. Admiral Collingwood to Erasmus Blackett, 7 November 1794, NRO, ZBL 247.

14. Lavery, *Nelsons Navy*, p.128.

15. Ibid.

16. The changing character of the Royal Navy and conditions of service in the second half of the eighteenth century can be followed in Rodger, N.A.M. 'Shipboard Life in the Georgian Navy, 1750-1800: The Decline of the Old Order?' in *The North Sea: Twelve Essays on Social History of Maritime Labour*, Fischer, L.R., Hamre, H., Holm, P. and Bruijn, J.R. Stavanger Maritime Museum/Association of North Sea Societies (Stavanger,1992).

17. Rodger, *Shipboard Life*, p. 35.

18. Hay, M.D. (ed.) *Landsman Hay: The Memoirs of Robert Hay, 1789-1847*, (London 1958), p. 66.

19. Manwaring, G.E. and Dobree, B. *Mutiny: The Floating Republic*, The Cresset Library (London, 1987), p. 10.

20. Dugan, J. *The Great Mutiny*, Andre Deutsch Ltd. (London, 1966), pp. 108-109.

21. Aaron Graham to Home Office, 12 May 1797, NA, ADM1/ 4172.

22. Ibid.

23. Manwaring and Dobree, *Mutiny*, Appendix 1.

24. These were *Sandwich*: William Robinson, aged 39, Yeoman of Sheets, South Shields whose record was endorsed 'a doubtful character'; Thomas Perkins, aged 26, Quartermaster's Mate, Durham; Thomas Thompson, aged 24, able seaman, North Shields; William Lambton, aged 40, able seaman, Sunderland; Thomas Weatherhead, aged 26, able seaman, Newcastle; NA, ADM36/11622. *Monmouth*: James Mandlon, aged 37, able seaman, Durham; Thomas Hunter, aged 25, Quartermaster's Mate, Newcastle; Joseph Grundy, aged 26, able seaman, Newcastle; Richard Bagnell, aged 20, ordinary seaman, Newcastle; NA, ADM36/ 12752. *Inflexible*: James Ross, aged 26, Quartermaster's Yeoman, Newcastle; Jonathan Nixon, aged 25, Quartermaster's Mate, Willington Quay; William Reed, aged 35, Quartermaster's Yeoman, Shields; Joseph Turner, aged 20, able seaman, Durham; NA, ADM36/12741.

25. NA, ADM1/5486.

26. Manwaring and Dobree, *Mutiny*, p. 327.

27. Muster books of *Mars*, NA, ADM 36/12233 & 12234 and ADM 6/98.

28. Sutherland, G. *The Whaling Years: Peterhead 1788-1893*, Centre for Scottish Studies, University of Aberdeen, (Aberdeen, 1993), pp. 6-7.

29. *H.M.S. Vanguard at the Nile: The Men, the Ship, the Battle*, The Nelson Society (1998).

30. Lubbock, B. *The Arctic Whalers*, Brown Son & Ferguson (Glasgow, 1937), p. 48.

31. Irwin, G. *Narrative of the Voyages and Adventures of George Irwin, a native of Hexham, during ten years in the Navy and Merchant Service, written by himself.* Dickinson, M. (Hexham, 1830), p. 46.

'Once more [I] beg your friendship in getting me clear of this
miserable situation for this is one of the most miserablist lives that ever
a man led.'

[Benjamin Stevenson of Berwick, Quartermaster,
HMS Victory August 1805]

Press Gangs

Few aspects of Nelson's navy have greater notoriety in popular
imagination than the press gang. Its clandestine activities were
universally condemned as an unjust and inefficient method of
manning the navy but in the absence of viable alternatives there
was little else the government could do. Pressing seamen was an
age-old practice and its legality was hardly disputed even by those
who became its principal victims. 'Prest' originally denoted a
monetary payment akin to the 'King's shilling'. It was first recorded
at Newcastle in 1543 when an entry in the Newcastle Trinity House
accounts noted expenses incurred '…when the mariner was prest
to go in the *Elizabeth*.'[1] Until the end of the seventeenth century
impressment was regarded as a piecemeal affair, either undertaken
on a temporary basis to crew individual ships or find enough seamen
to man the fleet during the summer months. By the middle of
the eighteenth century, however, the Impress Service was organised
on a semi-permanent basis and involved the employment of
hundreds of officers and men. Most of the principal ports had a

Regulating Captain who co-ordinated the activities of several gangs under his control from a Rendezvous, (or Rondy as it was popularly known), usually a large alehouse or tavern rented for the purpose.[2] Newcastle had a press gang of at least twenty men and there were gangs of a similar size at Shields and Sunderland. A commissioned officer, usually a lieutenant but sometimes an elderly or disabled captain, commanded each of these gangs.

In March 1803 Captain Adam Mackenzie was appointed as Regulating Captain at Newcastle. He was charged with the responsibility of rebuilding an effective organisation for impressment on the Tyne and Wear and reconstituting the gangs so hastily dismantled the year before. Mackenzie worked quickly and with the cooperation of the Common Council and constables of Newcastle, together with the crew of *Lapwing,* a frigate which happened to be lying in the river, he was able to carry out a first sweep for seamen within a fortnight of his arrival. It proved to be a disappointing start and few seamen were found. Most of them fled into the countryside on hearing a rumour that a press was likely to take place. Reinforcements arrived from the Admiralty in early April when Lieutenant John Mitchell was appointed to lead the press gang at Shields. About the same time, Mackenzie himself appointed a Lieutenant Bounton, then living locally on half-pay, to lead a gang at Sunderland.[3]

The arrival of press gangs naturally aroused considerable hostility and their activities soon provoked a number of stiff fights. Initially, Bounton found it impossible to establish a gang at Sunderland obliging Mackenzie to write:

> Lieutenant Bounton has this instant come away from
> Sunderland to inform me that he durst not attempt to
> impress at that place last night, as Mobs of hundreds

of Seamen, Soldiers and Women, got around the Rendezvous and threatened the lives of himself and People, whether they acted or not.[4]

Mackenzie expressed particular disappointment in the failure of local magistrates to support Bounton in his work and with the backing of the Home Office was able to threaten the withdrawal of all protections against impressment at Sunderland unless the magistrates acted more decisively. The tactic worked and the press gang at Sunderland soon established its presence in the town, although Bounton proved to be an ineffective leader and was later replaced. Mitchell was more successful although he too experienced considerable opposition, especially in South Shields where he was:

> Attacked by a Multitude of Pilots and Women, who threw a quantity of Stones and Brickbats at him, they likewise threatened to hew him down with their Spades, which are very dangerous Weapons…and likewise threatened to Murder him if ever he came back.[5]

After several further attempts, Mitchell eventually gained a foothold in South Shields but it was never a comfortable place for the gang to operate. Nevertheless, despite these difficulties Mackenzie successfully rebuilt the Impress Service to such an extent that by May 1803 press gangs were able to make regular sweeps for seamen at every port between Blyth and Sunderland.

As the threat of a Napoleonic invasion mounted the Admiralty resorted to a 'press from protections' in a desperate attempt to recruit more men but it met with little success on Tyneside. Most of the seamen entitled to receive protection certificates such as the 'Greenlanders', for example, were already at sea and on the whaling grounds. Other categories of protected seamen like carpenters and mates of colliers could not be pressed in numbers without disrupting the coal trade. However, since Press Warrants authorised Regulating Officers to take men '…whose occupations and callings are to work in vessels and boats upon rivers…' as well as merchant seamen, Mackenzie was determined to impress some of the keelmen, another group of protected mariners. It was a dangerous gamble and likely to provoke a political as well as an economic response. The keelmen manned the heavy sailing barges that carried coal from collieries in the upper reaches of the Tyne and Wear to colliers moored in the lower harbour at Shields and Sunderland. They were a well organised group of river workers and vital to the economy of the coal trade. In May 1803 Mackenzie pressed fifty-three keelmen on the river Tyne and shipped them off to *Zealand,* receiving ship at the Nore. The response was immediate; the coal trade came to a standstill. Local MPs and leading merchants hastened to London for discussions with the Admiralty in an attempt to resolve the dispute and secure the keelmen's release. They eventually succeeded in negotiating an agreement that restored protection to the keelmen in return for providing a quota of recruits amounting to one seaman or two landsmen for every ten protected keelmen. A similar agreement was concluded with the keelmen of the Wear in February 1804.[6]

Few of the victims of Mackenzie's experiment benefited from these arrangements and secured their release. Many even decided to volunteer in order to qualify for a bounty payment. Some of these keelmen were amongst two hundred 'volunteers' received by Collingwood into *Venerable* in September 1803. When that ship was wrecked off the Devonshire coast in December twenty-five men transferred to *Prince* all of whom were destined to fight at Trafalgar. There was at least one keelman, John Watson from Dunston, then aged twenty-eight. Watson survived Trafalgar and served in the navy until 1815. He lived long enough to claim a pension from Greenwich Hospital and his Trafalgar medal.[7] Other keelmen appear to have served on *Africa* [64], *Britannia* [100] and *Phoebe* [36].[8]

However, the largest number of North Country mariners to serve on a single ship at Trafalgar were those drafted to *Colossus* [74], a new ship built at Deptford and launched in April 1803. *Colossus* was launched soon after the outbreak of the same 'hot press' from which George Irwin had so narrowly escaped after royal marines boarded *Hercules* at Woolwich and pressed two men. Many of the seamen captured that night and during the weeks that followed it, found themselves drafted to *Colossus*. The first batch, entered into the muster book during June-July 1803, included a dozen 'Geordies' pressed from colliers in the Thames. The majority of them, like Robert Jackson of South Shields, aged twenty-one, and George Rule of Newcastle, aged twenty, were rated able seamen. Hardin Hall, aged forty-five and from Sunderland, was an old salt by comparison. He was just the kind of experienced seaman the navy was on the lookout for. Hall was raised to petty officer rank and rated quartermaster. A further thirty-five seamen from North East England were drafted to *Colossus* from *Zealand* at the Nore and entered into the muster book on 2 August 1803. Amongst them were seven of the keelmen pressed by Mackenzie at Newcastle in May. Three other 'Geordies', including George Trewhitt from Shields joined *Colossus* at Plymouth before she sailed to join the Channel Fleet.[9] *Colossus* eventually carried over fifty North Country seamen into action at Trafalgar.

Victory, Nelson's flagship, carried thirty-eight men from North East England. More than half of them had been impressed from colliers and other shipping that happened to be lying in the river Thames in April-May 1803. Amongst them was Benjamin Stevenson, pressed at Woolwich from an inbound collier and entered into *Victory's* muster book on 11 May 1803. Despite his promotion from able seaman to quartermaster, Stevenson was unimpressed with naval life and seemed indifferent to the privilege of serving on Nelson's ship. He expressed his concern in a letter to his brother at Newcastle written from *Victory* in August 1805 after the unsuccessful 'chase' of Villeneuve's fleet to the West Indies:

> Thank God for it my dear brother we have once more arrived in England and once more beg your friendship in getting me clear of this miserable situation… for this is one of the miserablest lives that ever a man led.[10]

Numerous other seamen taken by press gangs in similar circumstances to Stevenson were drafted to *Mars* [74], *Minotaur*, *Defence* [74], *Conqueror* [74] and *Tonnant*.

During February-March 1804 press gangs on Tyneside despatched almost 250 seamen to the receiving ship at the Nore. Many of them were entered as volunteers under the substitutes agreement made with the keelmen, others were taken forcibly. Not all of these new recruits were prime seamen and some were clearly of little value to the fleet. Collingwood writing from *Culloden* off Ushant in July 1804 observed:

> I have got a nurseryman here from Wrighton [Ryton]…it is a great pity that they should press such a man because when he was young he went to sea for a short time. They have broken up his good business at home, distressed his family and sent him here where he is of little or no service. I grieve for him, poor man![11]

The anonymous subject of Collingwood's observations probably reflected the experience of hundreds of other men around the country. Robert Arrowsmith, a ship's carpenter seized by a press gang during the summer of 1803, was a family man with seven children. Despite the active intervention of his friends and the pleadings of the mayor of Newcastle on his behalf, Arrowsmith was never released. In January 1804, George Davidson, mate of a vessel lying in the river Tyne, was seized by a press gang whilst drinking in a public house at 9 p.m. Charleton, the Regulating Captain at Newcastle confirmed his detention on the grounds that Davidson could not possibly have been ashore on ship's business![12] A notorious case of cruelty and injustice concerned the demise of John Babbington Stoddart.

Stoddart was an apprentice ship's carpenter hardly out of his teens and, as such, was entitled to protection from impressment. Nevertheless, he was forced to serve in the navy for a short time at the end of the French Revolutionary War but eventually released in August 1802. Stoddart returned to his native Tyneside and mustered to a Greenland whaler in March 1803 although seven of the crew were impressed at Shields before the ship was cleared to sail to the whaling grounds. Stoddart escaped on this occasion but appears to have fallen victim to a press gang soon after his return from the Arctic. In January 1804 he wrote to his mother from *Lynx* anchored at the Nore:

Dear Mother,

I am sorry to inform you that I had the misfortune to be presst [sic] yesterday from want of my indentures for my servitude as a carpenter. So if you please to send my indentures and bond to Mr. Bishop as soon as possible he will do his endeavours as far as lays in his power. I told Mr. Bishop if it was £20 he was not to mind the expense.[13]

Stoddart's investment secured his release and he made his way back to Tyneside. However, as soon as he stepped ashore on Newcastle Quayside the press gang gave chase. In a desperate bid to escape Stoddart jumped into the Tyne and struck out for the Gateshead shore. He was shot dead by an infuriated member of the gang. A coroner's inquest concluded that Stoddart '…lost his presence of mind and was drowned'.[14] The circumstances of Stoddart's murder were, no doubt, exceptional but death or serious injury was by no means unique. Older members of Tyneside communities in 1804 would certainly have remembered the *Noble Ann* Affair of 1779 when two whalermen were killed and another seriously wounded by a press gang at Shields. A similar incident involving the crew of a Hull whaler, *Sarah and Elizabeth,* had occurred off the Humber ten years before.[15]

Greenland whalermen, despite their protected status, were prime targets of the press gang and many of them were forcibly recruited into the navy between 1803 and 1805. Arctic whalers carried crews of forty or fifty men who were vulnerable to impressment on the homeward voyage at the end of the whaling season. Fourteen men were pressed from the Whitby whaler *Henrietta* in 1804 and so many Greenlanders were pressed from the London bound whaler *Ocean* off the Humber the owners considered that it had endangered the safe navigation of the ship. They brought a case in the Court of Kings Bench in 1804 that established the illegality of pressing Greenland seamen, but it had little practical effect.[16] In July 1806 twelve men were pressed from *John and Margaret,* a veteran whaler from Shields, by boats from *Druid* [36]. Ironically, *Druid* had been sent to Orkney to protect the whaling fleet from attack by French privateers.[17]

Seamen with Arctic whaling experience may well have been amongst those who were drafted to *Revenge*, the newest ship to fight at Trafalgar. *Revenge* was launched at Deptford in April 1805. Captain Robert Moorsom, son of a Whitby whaler owner, appears to have attracted a number of seamen from the region. There were eight Whitby-born men amongst thirty mariners and royal marines from North East England serving on *Revenge,* many of them pressed and drafted into the ship from *Zealand* at the Nore in June-July 1805. The captain's young son, Constantine R.

Moorsom, also appears in the muster book of *Revenge* as a volunteer, first class.[18]

Pressing seamen from ships at sea was the preferred method of most naval officers because it represented the most effective means of securing experienced seamen for the fleet. The sheer volume of regional shipping trading regularly to London at the beginning of the nineteenth century made the navy's task easier, particularly for warships allocated to coastal patrol and convoy protection in the North Sea. Robert Arrowsmith, for example, appears to have been one of a number of men pressed by boats from *Cruizer* off the coast of North East England. Ten of these men were subsequently drafted to *Minotaur* in April 1803.[19] Captain Hope of *Defence*, newly re-commissioned with orders to join the North Sea detachment of the Channel Fleet in 1803, took the opportunity to complete his crew by stopping and boarding numerous London-bound colliers off the coast of Suffolk. 'Either by volunteering or by impressment we procured upwards of a hundred able seamen all of whom proved to be not only excellent sailors but a very orderly and well-behaved crew.'[20]

Defence subsequently carried twenty-seven seamen from the region into action at Trafalgar, most of them 'Geordies' recruited off the east coast of England during the summer of 1803. Experienced seamen were vulnerable to this kind of impressment almost anywhere. Captain John Loring of *Bellerophon* pressed fourteen men from ships in a homeward bound Jamaica convoy in July 1803. Amongst them was Richard Nicholson, a thirty-five year old shipwright from Blyth and John Fox, a twenty-seven year old able seaman from Whitby. *Bellerophon*'s muster book shows that both men were pressed from *Theseus* on 23 July 1803.[21] They served at Trafalgar together with twelve other seamen from the region. Nicholson was subsequently promoted to warrant officer rank in 1807 as a carpenter, and served in the ship until the end of the Napoleonic War.

Bellerophon returned to England from the West Indies in August 1804 and went into dock at Portsmouth where she was re-coppered and refitted for a total cost of almost £12,000.[22] *Bellerophon* lost two 'Geordies', David Meldrum from Newcastle and Thomas Chisholm from Shields, who ran from the ship before she sailed to join the Channel Fleet, but gained two officers whose subsequent exploits made them household names.[23] They were William Pryce Cumby, a new first lieutenant, who fought with distinction at Trafalgar and a young midshipman, John Franklin, who later became famous as an Arctic explorer.

When news of Villeneuve's escape from Toulon reached England in May 1805 *Bellerophon* was ordered to the Straits of Gibraltar as part of a squadron commanded by Cuthbert Collingwood in *Dreadnought* [98]. The Admiral's flag captain was Edward Rotheram. More is known about individual members of the crew of *Bellerophon* than almost any other ship at Trafalgar, principally because of detailed descriptions and biographical notes compiled by the captain of *Bellerophon* between 1805 and 1808. The officer responsible for this remarkable piece of evidence was the same Edward Rotheram. Collingwood appointed him to *Bellerophon* after her former captain, John Cooke, was killed at Trafalgar.[24]

References

1. Ostler and Barrow, *Tall Ships*, p. 34.

2. Lavery, *Nelson's Navy*, pp. 120-121.

3. McCord, N. 'The Impress Service in North East England during the Napoleonic War', Mariners Mirror, vol. 54 (1968), in *Press Gangs and Privateers: Aspects of the Maritime History of North East England*, Barrow, T. (ed.), The Bewick Press (Whitley Bay, 1993), p. 24.

4. McCord, *Impress Service*, p. 25.

5. McCord, *Impress Service*, p. 26. The reference to "spades which are very dangerous weapons", is an interesting one and may relate to the implements used by pitmen and coal trimmers. I am grateful to Professor McCord for drawing my attention to this reference.

6. Ibid.

7. NA, ADM 36/15636-40 derived from the Ayshford Complete Trafalgar Roll.

8. These were the men who gave Blaydon, Swalwell and Dunstan as their place of birth, all well-established keelmen's communities on the river Tyne in this period. See NA, ADM 36/15825 (*Colossus*); ADM 37/99 (*Africa*); ADM 36/15996 (*Britannia*); ADM 36/15677 (*Phoebe*). Muster books of *Africa*, *Britannia* and *Phoebe* derived from Ayshford Complete Trafalgar Roll.

9. NA, ADM 36/15825.

10. National Maritime Museum (NMM) ref. BGY/T/1 cited in Lavery, B. *Nelson's Fleet at Trafalgar*, NMM, (London, 2004), p. 86.

11. Admiral Collingwood to Erasmus Blackett, 20 July 1804, Newnham-Collingwood, G.L. *A Selection from the Public and Private Correspondence of Vice-Admiral Lord Collingwood*, James Ridgeway (London, 1829), Letter 55, p. 96.

12. McCord, *Impress Service*, pp. 29-30. Protection certificates issued to the principal officers of merchant ships usually allowed them to transact business and undertake administrative duties ashore as long as they could demonstrate

that it concerned the ship or its owners. Davidson's 'offence' could hardly be construed as either business or duties.

13. Haswell, G.H. *The Maister: A Century of Tyneside Life*, Walter Scott (London, 1896), p. 63.

14. Haswell, *The Maister*, pp. 63-64.

15. Barrow, *Press Gangs and Privateers*, p. 22.

16. Ibid.

17. NA, ADM 36/17072.

18. NA, ADM 36/16546. Whether Constantine R. Moorsom actually served on *Revenge* at Trafalgar is unclear. It was common practice for the son of a serving officer to be borne on the ship's books whilst the young man was still at school.

19. NA, ADM 36/16227 derived from the Ayshford Complete Trafalgar Roll.

20. Lavery, *Nelson's Fleet*, p. 58.

21. NA, ADM 36/16498.

22. Cordingly, *Billy Ruffian*, Appendix 2.

23. NA, ADM 36/16498.

24. NMM, LBK/38, 'The Letters of Captain Edward Rotheram 1799-1830', cited in Lavery, *Nelson's Fleet*, p. 43.

'I must tell you what a squeeze we had…we drew off towards the Straits, not very ambitious as you may suppose, to try our strength against such odds.'

[Admiral Collingwood to Sarah Collingwood,
25 August 1805]

The Cadiz Squadron

The sequence of events that culminated at Trafalgar in October 1805 was set in train more than a year before. On his return to office as Prime Minister in May 1804, William Pitt, with Castlereagh's diplomacy, assembled a third anti-French coalition of powers consisting of Britain, Russia, Austria and Sweden. At the same time Pitt put pressure on Spain to relinquish its policy of providing assistance to France. Napoleon for his part, recognising the trend of British policy, determined to pre-empt it by staging his long-planned invasion of England in 1805. Success in the venture was dependent either upon a decisive naval victory over the British Channel Fleet, which seemed unlikely, or, an elaborate subterfuge designed to lure a sufficient number of warships away from the Channel Fleet for long enough to give France a temporary superiority in the English Channel. Both options depended upon the cooperation of Spain and this Pitt was determined to prevent. Accordingly, in October 1804 the Admiralty extended the blockade responsibilities of the Channel

Fleet by creating a Cadiz squadron and appointed Vice-Admiral Sir John Orde to command it. Orde was instructed to:

> Proceed as expeditiously as possible off Cadiz and cruise off that port for the purpose of watching the ships of war which may be lying there...and if you fall in with any ships laden with treasure coming from the Spanish colonies and bound for Spain you are to take possession of the said ships.[1]

Fearing that Spanish wealth would fall into French hands, four Spanish treasure ships were intercepted by British frigates west of Cadiz on 3 October 1804. In the ensuing action three ships were captured and the other blew up and sank with heavy loss of life, including women and children. Spain protested at such blatant provocation and declared war on Britain in December. An alliance between Spain and France quickly followed. Paradoxically, Pitt's policy had provoked the very alliance he had hoped to prevent. The Spanish ships were estimated to be worth one million pounds and brought instant wealth in prize money to the naval officers involved. It was especially fortuitous for Sir John Orde who did not arrive off Cadiz to take active command of the squadron until November. He may have felt that his good fortune was just recompense for the humiliations he had suffered at the hands of Spencer, First Lord of the Admiralty, and Admiral Earl St. Vincent in 1798.

Sir John Orde (1751-1824) was born at Nunnykirk near Morpeth, the son of a Northumberland landowner with extensive estates in the county. He entered the navy in 1766 and was promoted rapidly for his distinguished service in North America during the War of Independence. He became a post-captain in 1778 at the age of twenty-six, and served as Governor of Dominica from 1783-1793. Orde's attempts to secure an active command after the outbreak of the French Revolutionary War were repeatedly frustrated by bad luck and the obstructionism of Lord Spencer with whom Orde had a strained relationship. In 1795 Orde was raised to flag-rank as Rear-Admiral of the White in a general promotion of serving officers. As Admiral commanding at Plymouth in 1797, Sir John Orde was praised for his judicious handling of a mutiny there and, probably because of it, he was appointed as presiding officer at the courts martial of the ringleaders of the mutiny at the Nore, where he gained widespread respect for his handling of the trials. In recognition, Orde was appointed to command *Princess Royal* [98] and sailed out to join St. Vincent patrolling off Cadiz in October 1797 as third in command. It was the apogee of his naval career.

In April 1798 when it seemed certain that a French expeditionary force was preparing to sail from Toulon for an undisclosed destination in the Mediterranean, St. Vincent was ordered to detach a squadron of ships to go in pursuit of it. Horatio Nelson was appointed to command the squadron despite Sir John's seniority to him on the Navy List. Orde protested vehemently that Nelson's appointment impugned his abilities and his honour. St. Vincent claimed that his orders had come directly from the Admiralty and that he had no choice in the matter, but it sowed the seeds of resentment and distrust and his relationship with Admiral Orde broke down irretrievably over the weeks that followed. To make matters worse the arrival of Admiral Sir Roger Curtis's squadron from Ireland had the effect of demoting Orde to fourth in command. In June 1798 an exasperated St. Vincent relieved Sir John Orde of his command and sent him back to England in disgrace. It was almost unprecedented for a commander-in-chief to dismiss a senior admiral without first consulting the Admiralty. St. Vincent was severely reprimanded for his action and it provoked considerable sympathy for the perceived injustice done to Orde. Collingwood, who had always been on good terms with St. Vincent, expressed a view shared by a number of senior officers:

It seemed to everybody an unwarrantable stretch of
power...without the slightest degree of misdemeanour.
Sir John Orde is proud and carries himself
high...[but]...it needed not great sensibility to feel
injustice [and] these were generally gross enough even
for the roughest minds...he treated Sir John Orde very
ill.[2]

Sir John's appointment to command the Cadiz squadron in
October 1804 was his first sea-going command since the spat
with Admiral St. Vincent six years before. Unfortunately it also
turned out to be his last. When Villeneuve sailed from Toulon on
30 March 1805 with eleven ships of the line and eight other
warships, Nelson's squadron was watering in Sardinia ignorant of
this crucial development. Villeneuve's passage through the Straits
of Gibraltar ten days later caught Orde's squadron completely off
guard. It was a flat calm and almost every ship had a transport
alongside. *Agamemnon* was unrigged with the main yard sent
down and her decks littered with casks and naval stores. As soon
as Sir John received a report of the imminent approach of the
French fleet he ordered the transports cast off and his ships cleared
for action. Outnumbered almost three to one the Cadiz squadron
withdrew to the south rather than risk a battle and, believing that
Villeneuve's fleet was intended as the covering force for Napoleon's
invasion, sailed north to reinforce the Channel fleet. In the absence
of contrary information it was a sensible decision. However, Orde
was castigated for the timidity of his response, censored for
omitting to detach a frigate to shadow the French to establish its
destination and criticised for his failure to inform Nelson that the
Toulon fleet was at sea.

In the flurry of activity surrounding the Admiralty's response
to the developing situation Orde's request to retire, which pre-
dated the crisis then unfolding, was finally accepted. He struck
his flag in *Glory* [98] at Spithead on 10 May 1805. The timing

could not have been worse. Orde, conscious that his retirement was being misconstrued as a dismissal 'to calumniate and disgrace me in the public estimation',[3] requested a court martial, for the second time in his career, as a means of explaining his decision to withdraw from Cadiz and clear his name. The Admiralty refused Sir John's request and despite his efforts he was never given another command at sea.

When the Franco-Spanish Combined Fleet finally returned to Cadiz after the failure of its Atlantic diversion, it found Collingwood patrolling off the port with only three ships of the line, *Dreadnought, Colossus* and *Achille* [74]. Facing impossible odds he was forced to retire towards Gibraltar

> I must tell you what a squeeze we had...While we were cruising off the town, down came the Combined Fleet of thirty-six men of war; we were only three poor little things with a frigate and a bomb and we drew off towards the Straits, not very ambitious, as you may suppose, to try our strength against such odds.[4]

Once his squadron had gained a safe distance, Collingwood sent his fastest ship *Colossus* back towards Cadiz to observe the movements of Villeneuve's fleet. The following day a frigate arrived with the intelligence that the Combined Fleet was on its way! Collingwood already knew. He dispatched the same frigate to England with the news and set about building his fleet before Villeneuve realised its numerical weakness.

By August 1805 *Dreadnought* had been Collingwood's flagship for almost a year. She was a relatively new warship completed at Portsmouth in 1801 and was the ship that brought the admiral together with Edward Rotheram. Like many flag-captains, Rotheram was a comparatively inexperienced commanding officer whose previous command had been a frigate, *Lapwing,* from 1800-

1802.[5] It was usual for an admiral of Collingwood's standing to have some choice in the selection of his flag-captain but Rotheram appears to have been appointed to *Dreadnought* independently of Collingwood's preference. It proved to be an unhappy liaison and the two men endured a difficult relationship for almost a year, despite their shared adversity. In appointing Rotheram the Admiralty probably believed they were satisfying Collingwood's known preference for officers from his native Newcastle whilst at the same time enabling him to maintain an independent command since, 'Custom permitted an Admiral to interfere a good deal in the internal management of his flagship'.[6] As it turned out, Collingwood was obliged to shoulder rather more responsibility for the management of *Dreadnought* than he had bargained for. His correspondence consistently reflected his irritation with Rotheram as well as his low opinion of his captain's temperament and abilities. He wrote to his cousin Edward Collingwood in September 1805, 'I have a gentleman from Newcastle as my captain but he is a man of no talent as a sea officer and of very little assistance to me, so that the full weight of everything lays on me'[7], and in a letter to his sister written a few days after his brush with the Combined Fleet off Cadiz, Collingwood complained:

> Clavell, my Lieutenant, is the spirit of the ship; but such a captain, such a stick, I wonder how such people get forward. Was he brought up in the Navy? For he has very much the stile (sic) of the coal trade about him, except that they are good seamen.[8]

These were damning indictments of Rotheram's manner and style of ship management, as well as his seamanship, and Collingwood did nothing to disguise his opinions from other officers. Many years later, Hercules Robinson, then a young midshipman, recalled an incident on the quarterdeck of *Dreadnought* when Collingwood, having observed another of his

Mouth of the Tyne *by J. S. Swift* c. 1859
A scene off Shields Bar about 1830. The vessel in the foreground, surrounded by fishing boats, adjusts sails on arrival off Tynemouth while in the distance an outward-bound collier is towed to sea by a paddle tug. *Tyne and Wear Museums.*

North Shore, Newcastle *J. W. Carmichael.*
A riverside scene familiar to Keelmen in the 1820s, close to where the Gateshead Millennium Bridge now stands.

Low Lights, North Shields *J.W. Carmichael.*
A crowded harbour scene about 1830. The scullerboats (ferry boats) in the foreground often provided a livelihood for 'Trafalgar Geordies' in their old age.

The protection certificate of John Ramsey, aged seventeen, a keelman on the river Wear. It was issued in January 1806 under the substitutes agreement with the Admiralty. The certificate confirms that Ramsay had subscribed to 'the expense of hiring and retaining Robert Smith as a volunteer to serve in His Majesty's Navy…as a substitute for Ten Keelmen at this Port'.

Contemporary illustrations of keelmen reveal their distinctive occupational dress. Later, they adopted naval fashions for their walking-out dress including 'man-o-war' trousers.

After 1803 the Keelmen agreed to provide an annual quota of recruits for the navy equivalent to one tenth of their numbers. A similar agreement was reached with the Wear Keelmen in 1804.

A Keelmen getting his orders
Tyne & Wear Museums.

Keelmen playing at cards
Tyne & Wear Museums.

The brig *Margaret* by *John Scott c. 1845*
'Geordie' brigs were the mainstays of the coal trade in the age of sail and the type of vessel in which thousands of local seamen learnt their skills.
Tyne & Wear Museums.

Friends and Fellow Seamen!

THE Affociation has offered a Bounty of One Guinea a Man, in Addition to his Majefty's Bounty, to induce us to enter on Board his Majefty's Ships of War;—but Bounties, however large they may appear at firft, do not laft long; and when they are expended in Cloaths and other Neceffaries, we are obliged to live upon the fame Pay as before, which we well know from Experience we cannot live upon.—What then is intended by this feeming Kindnefs? Evidently to induce us to engage ourfelves to ruin our Families, to lofe our Limbs or Lives; and at the End of a War, which, from all we can learn, is at leaft unne-ceffary, to be paid off, or, in other Words, to be turned adrift, at a Diftance from our Friends, without the Means of procuring an honeft Livelihood:—Befides, does not this Offer of additional Bounty plainly fhew, that the Affociation and others are of Opinion that our prefent Pay is not fufficient? Elfe why do they offer it? We have always fhewn a Readinefs to meet the Enemies of our Country, fo that our prefent Objections do not proceed from Cowardice, but from the dreadful Miferies which we have known, feen, and felt, in our Families and Connections; there we cannot confcientioufly, either as Men, Britons, or Chriftians, any longer countenance by Compliance, fuch a fhocking Abufe of Power.—Twenty-two fhillings a Month, Fellow-Seamen, is Five Shillings a week! A Sum too fmall for even a fingle Man to live upon; but many of us have Wives and Familes, many others, Sifters, and other Relations, whofe very Exiftence depends upon our Lives and Succefs: From thefe we are torn and compelled to accept this fmall Sum, which is not Half what we receive in the Merchants' Service: Is not this very hard? None of us choofe a life of War: And if we are fuch Friends to our Countrymen that we are always ready to ftep forward in their Defence, why fhould our Situa-tion in Time of War be rendered fo much worfe than in Time of Peace? We can then live comfortably, fupport our Families decently, give our Children an honeft and ufeful Education, and make them good and worthy Members of Society.—In Time of War we cannot, from the miferably fmall Pay, even live ourfelves. But this is not the worft,—our Children and Dependents are neglected: They are expofed to all the Miferies of Poverty, and are hindered in their Courfe of Life by Want of Protection and Education. Thefe are great Calamities; and it is to remedy thefe, not to create Difturbances, that we defire you to confider ferioufly thefe Grievances: but tho' we hope they will be redreffed, yet in order to attain fo defirable an End, we will preferve Peace and Order; we will not by Violence fhall difgrace the Conduct of Men who are engaged in fo good a Caufe as that in which we are engaged; and when we only feek the fame Rights of Protection from feemingly abufed Power, as the of our Fellow-citizens, we doubt not but we fhall be aided by every good and ous Man in the Kingdom.

Newcaftle, February 2, 1793.

A Broadsheet published in Newcastle at the outbreak of the French Revolutionary War. It explains the grievances of merchant seamen concerning wages and conditions in the Royal Navy. They became the basis of the seamen's demands during the mutiny at Spithead in 1797. *Newcastle Central Library (Local Studies).*

A COLLIER, WITH A VIEW OF THE SOUTH FORELAND. VUE D'UN NAVIRE CHARBONNIER, ET DE SOUTH FORELAND.

The Thames Estuary could be a dangerous place for merchant seamen in the age of Press Gangs. In these scenes the artist *Serres* depicts a collier (above) and a warship (below) within a few miles of each other off the Kentish coast.

A SHIP OF THE LINE IN THE DOWNS. VUE D'UN VAISSEAU DE GUERRE DANS LES DUNES.

Cove of South Shields, whaling in Baffin Bay, c.1830. *George Palmer Collection. Courtesy of Stephen Wolfenden.*
Despite their status as protected seamen 'Greenlanders' were regularly impressed at sea as they returned from the whaling grounds.

captain's crass blunders called Rotheram to him and caustically observed:

> Captain, I have been thinking whilst I looked at you, how strange that a man who has grown so big should know so little....that's all Sir.[9]

Collingwood's correspondence was more positive about William Landless, a Northumberland-born lieutenant of *Dreadnought* who had joined the ship from *Venerable* in August 1804. Landless had been a lieutenant since 1796 and he followed Collingwood from ship to ship for many years in the expectation that the Admiral would be able to advance his naval career. In addition to Landless and other officers, there were nineteen seamen from North East England amongst the crew of *Dreadnought,* which represented about 3 per cent of her complement. George Duncan, a twenty-one year old able seaman from Newcastle transferred to the ship from *Venerable* at the same time as Landless, whereas Henry Potts from South Shields, another able seaman, had been pressed at Southampton in 1803.[10]

When Nelson arrived off Cadiz he found Collingwood's squadron stronger and more prepared than it had been two months before. Nelson asked him to remain as second-in-command and shift his flag from *Dreadnought* to *Royal Sovereign.* Initially Collingwood seemed reluctant to comply; *Royal Sovereign* was a much older ship completed in 1786 and amongst the first warships to be mobilised at the outbreak of the French Wars. She took part in the battle of the Glorious First of June in 1794 and had seen much active service ever since. Collingwood knew that *Royal Sovereign* had developed a reputation as a slow sailer but was unaware that the ship had recently undergone a refit that included the re-coppering of her hull. This work transformed her sailing qualities and enabled *Royal Sovereign* to move a few knots faster than her consorts in light winds, a quality that had significant consequences for her crew at Trafalgar.

It has long been assumed that *Royal Sovereign* carried a substantial number of seamen from North East England amongst her crew, largely because of Collingwood's known preference for them. Even the editors of contemporary local newspapers believed this to be true. In fact, *Royal Sovereign* carried only fourteen seamen and one royal marine from the region, about 1.5 per cent, a lower proportion of locally-born seamen than most other British ships of the line at Trafalgar. The average number of seamen per ship who were from North East England was eighteen, or 3 per cent, based on a crew of 600 men. These proportions varied enormously of course. *Neptune* [98] carried just four seamen from the region in a crew of over 700 men, less than 1 per cent. By contrast, seamen from Northumberland, Durham and the North Riding of Yorkshire represented 10 per cent of the crew of *Colossus* and in ships like *Victory, Prince, Revenge* and *Defence* about 6 per cent. Before *Royal Sovereign* arrived as part of Nelson's fleet she was affectionately known as the 'West Country Wagon' for her slow speed and established connections with Devon and Cornwall where 10 per cent of the crew had been born. These associations hardly changed when Collingwood shifted his flag to the ship on 11 October 1805. He took only a small retinue of officers with him including Rotheram as his flag-captain, which seemed a surprising choice in the circumstances, Clavell as his first lieutenant, George Castle, Grenville Thompson and several other midshipmen. James Graydon, a twenty-one year old quarter gunner from East Rainton near Durham, was also taken.[11] Collingwood had also intended to take William Landless as a second lieutenant but Landless was suffering from a medical condition affecting his eyes and the Admiral thought it best to leave him in *Dreadnought* until it cleared up. Collingwood had a reputation for training his seamen hard in gunnery and when he left *Dreadnought* for *Royal Sovereign* the crew were reputed to be able to fire three rounds in five minutes. Clavell, Graydon and the young midshipmen had just ten days to adjust to conditions in their new flagship and drill *Royal Sovereign's* crew in rapid-fire gunnery, to Collingwood's exacting standards, before the battle of Trafalgar[12].

References

1. Orde, D. *Nelson's Mediterranean Command,* The Pentland Press Ltd. (Bishop Auckland, 1997), p. 153-154.

2. Orde, *Nelson's Mediterranean Command,* p. 127-128. On his return to England Sir John requested a court martial on St. Vincent as a way of exonerating him from any blame in the affair but Lord Spencer, First Lord of the Admiralty, refused to allow it. When Admiral St. Vincent eventually returned to England in 1799 an exasperated Sir John Orde challenged his former commander-in-chief to a duel – but Sir John was bound over to keep the peace and it was never fought. Orde subsequently published the correspondence between himself and St. Vincent a copy of which is preserved at NRO (Gosforth) under Ref.1350/C.

3. Orde, *Nelson's Mediterranean Command,* p. 175.

4. Newnham-Collingwood, Admiral Collingwood to Sarah Collingwood, 25 August 1805, *Correspondence of Lord Collingwood,* p. 109.

5. NA, ADM 9/2/142.

6. Rodger, *The Wooden World,* p. 19.

7. Admiral Collingwood to Edward Collingwood, 23 September 1805, Duffy, M. (ed.), *Naval Miscellany,* vol.

VI, Ashgate for the Navy Records Society (London, 2003), Letter 14, p. 181.

8.   Staniforth, F. *Admiral Collingwood and his flag-captain on the Royal Sovereign, Edward Rotheram, North Magazine*, vol. 4 (October 1971), pp. 14-15.

9.   Lavery, *Nelson's Fleet*, p. 129.

10. Detail derived from Ayshford Complete Trafalgar Roll.

11. NA, ADM36/15754.

12. The names of seamen from North East England who served on *Royal Sovereign* and other warships at the Battle of Trafalgar can be found in Appendix One.

'I am come off safe without the least hurt except a deafness for a few days which has now gone off.'

[Robert Jackson of South Shields, able seaman,
H.M.S. Colossus]

The Battle of Trafalgar

Victory arrived off Cadiz on 28 September 1805 and in the days that followed Nelson explained the plan of attack to all of his captains. He first envisaged a fleet of forty ships organised into three divisions, two of sixteen ships and a mobile force of eight of his fastest warships stationed to respond to the circumstances of a developing battle. Since he could not know for certain the size of the Combined Fleet nor predict the strength or direction of the wind, his strategy was adaptable and he expected his captains to use their initiative. Nelson would lead the first division and cut through the enemy's line towards the centre a few ships ahead of the flagship. Collingwood's division was to attack about twelve ships from the enemy's rear.[1] The mobile squadron was to support the ships already engaged and attack where it could cause maximum damage. As it turned out Nelson had to settle for a smaller fleet than he had hoped for. On 19 October it consisted of twenty-seven ships of the line, four frigates and two smaller vessels. It meant that he had to dispense with his fast, mobile squadron. Collingwood's lee, or downwind column consisted of fifteen ships, and Nelson's weather, or windward column, numbered eleven ships. *Africa* which became separated from the main fleet during the night, joined the battle independently as part of Nelson's weather division.

As a way of concealing the strength of his main fleet Nelson posted three ships between himself and Cadiz to relay signalled information received from British frigates observing the preparations of Villeneuve's ships. *Defence* and *Colossus,* which between them carried over eighty seamen from North East England, were the closest inshore, while *Mars* provided the final link to Nelson. Blackwood, captain of the frigate *Euryalus,* reported increased activity amongst the ships of the Combined Fleet as early as 9 October but they did not leave Cadiz until the morning of Saturday 19 October. *Euryalus* made the signal to the Inshore Squadron and *Mars,* standing far out on the distant horizon, relayed it to Nelson in *Victory.* The first officer in the main fleet to recognise and interpret the signal was William Pryce Cumby, first lieutenant of *Bellerophon:*

> Early in the forenoon of Saturday 19th October…I perceived flags flying at the masthead of the lookout ship towards Cadiz the *Mars* and distinctly made out to my satisfaction the numerical signal 370 signifying, 'The enemy's ships are coming out of port or getting under weigh'.

Cumby reported the signal to his captain who hesitated to repeat it unless another officer could confirm Cumby's interpretation of it. None were able to do so and 'I had the mortification to be disappointed in my anxious wish the *Bellerophon* should be the first to repeat such delightful intelligence to the Admiral'.[2]

Believing that the Combined Fleet was heading for the Mediterranean, Nelson ordered a general chase towards Gibraltar but with light and variable winds there was little chance of closing with it and forcing a battle that day. Villeneuve reversed the course of his fleet during the night in the hope of deceiving the British but it was spotted and reported by Nelson's frigates and his main fleet altered course in response to the change.

All of the ships in Nelson's fleet prepared for action as they slowly closed the gap between themselves and the Combined Fleet. Hammocks were stowed in nets around the sides of the ship where they could afford some protection from splinters and sharpshooters. Furniture was removed from the wardroom and the wooden partitions, used to separate the officers' quarters from the men, were taken down and stowed. In *Tonnant* windsor chairs used in the wardroom, 'were suspended by rope passed from the main to the mizzen mast'.[3] All the gun decks were cleared to give maximum space and most of the gun crews spent another anxious night sleeping by their guns. Robert Jackson, on *Colossus* recalled:

> We lay by our guns all that night and on the Monday morning by grey daylight the *Agamemnon* and us, being on the lookout, we saw such a sight as rejoiced each Englishman's heart to look on.[4]

Cumby on *Bellerophon* stood the first watch between midnight and four in the morning:

> Without anything particular having occured through the night except the frequent burning of the blue lights and false fires by our frigates to leeward which assured us that the enemy was still seen by them. I again turned-in… when about a quarter before six I was aroused from my slumbers by my shipmate Overton the Master

who called out … 'Cumby my boy, turn out, here they are ready for you close under our lee and evidently disposed to await our attack'.[5]

In fact the Combined Fleet was still more than ten miles away and in such light winds the leading British ships might take six hours to reach it. Nevertheless, *Bellerophon*'s crew were called to readiness and final preparations were made. Cumby chose three petty officers to steer the ship into battle; two of them came from North East England. They were thirty-nine year old William Ferguson from North Shields who had served continuously in the Royal Navy since the outbreak of the French Wars in 1793, and John Stewart, a thirty-six year old quartermaster from Berwick with eleven years service. These men were amongst fourteen seamen from the region who served on board *Bellerophon* at Trafalgar.[6]

On *Royal Sovereign* Collingwood's journal recorded the sequence of events as the two fleets moved towards each other:

Mon. 21 October 1805

At daylight saw the enemy's fleet to leeward and at 6:30 the Commander-in-Chief made the signal to form the order of sailing in two columns and at 7:00 to prepare for battle. At 7:40 to bear-up east in which direction the enemy's fleet were forming their line. Bore-up, set the royals and made all sail towards the enemy. Made the signal for Tonnant and Belleisle to interchange places in the line the former ship not being able to keep up with Royal Sovereign.[7]

Jackson on *Colossus* recalled:

At six bells or eleven o'clock we were piped to dinner – every man had half a pint of wine, we were very near them; at half-past eleven the drum beat to quarters, each messmate shook hands and wished each other well and we went to our guns cheerfully.[8]

As the crew of *Colossus* went to their guns Nelson's famous signal, 'England expects that every man will do his duty', fluttered from the masthead of *Victory*. By this time with all of her sails set and a relatively clean, re-coppered hull, *Royal Sovereign* slowly moved ahead of other ships in the British line. Collingwood could be seen pacing up and down the break of the quarterdeck munching an apple, while Clavell, with Rotheram's permission, adjusted the sails and made some final checks on the readiness of the guns' crews. Just before noon the French ship *Fougueux* opened fire on *Royal Sovereign* now about a mile ahead of *Belleisle* the next ship in the lee column. These were the opening broadsides of the battle of Trafalgar. Cumby on *Bellerophon* watched as Collingwood's flagship came under sustained fire from several enemy warships. Eventually *Royal Sovereign* broke through the enemy's line between *Fougueux* and *Santa Ana* which carried the flag of the Spanish Admiral Alava. Collingwood's journal recorded:

> About noon the *Royal Sovereign* opened fire on the 12, 13, 14 and 15 ships from the enemy's rear and stood on with all sail to break the enemy's line. At quarter-past twelve altered course to port and in passing close under the stern of *Santa Ana*, a Spanish three-deck ship with a Vice-Admiral's flag raked her and sheering up on her starboard side began a very close action.[9]

Fougueux received the full weight of *Royal Sovereign's* double-shotted broadside as she passed through the enemy's line. Pierre Servaulx, an officer on the French ship recalled:

I thought the *Fougueux* was shattered to pieces –
pulverised. The storm of projectiles that hurled
themselves against and through the hull on the port
side made the ship heel to starboard. Most of the sails
and rigging were cut to pieces, while the upper deck
was swept clear of the greater number of the seamen
working there.[10]

Once through the enemy's line Collingwood's flagship became
dangerously exposed and paid the penalty for being so far ahead
of the other ships in the lee column. She suffered so much from
the fire of at least five enemy ships that Collingwood ordered his
marines to seek shelter from the murderous musketry then being
directed at *Royal Sovereign's* exposed decks. At one point, in the
early stages of the battle, only Collingwood and Rotheram
remained on the quarterdeck. When a junior officer advised that
Rotheram should make himself less conspicuous and remove his
hat, Rotheram dismissed the suggestion and replied 'I have always
fought in a cocked hat and I always will'.[11]

George Castle, the young midshipman from Durham, stationed
at one of the heavy 32-pounder guns on the lower gun deck
remembered, 'I looked once out of the stern ports but I saw nothing
but French and Spaniards round firing at us in all directions'.[12]

Castle later claimed that *Royal Sovereign* fought alone for almost
an hour before another British ship became engaged but this was
certainly an exaggeration and probably reflected Castle's heightened
emotional state. He was, after all, only sixteen years of age. *Royal
Sovereign* fought single-handed for about twenty minutes before
Belleisle broke through the enemy's line astern of *Fougueux*; *Mars*
and *Tonnant* arrived about ten minutes later. The windsor chairs
suspended in *Tonnant's* rigging were amongst the earliest casualties.
Bellerophon also joined the battle about 12:30. As she passed close

under the stern of the Spanish *Monarca* [74], *Bellerophon* fired two devastating broadsides into the Spanish ship but then collided with the French *L'Aigle* [74]. The yards and rigging of the two ships became entangled and a close ship-to-ship engagement soon developed. *L'Aigle* was a formidable opponent. She carried 150 soldiers who swept *Bellerophon's* decks with musketry and forced her royal marines to seek shelter. Captain Cooke was an obvious target and Cumby urged him to remove his distinctive epaulettes but Cooke refused and paid the ultimate price for his bravery. At precisely 1.11 according to *Bellerophon's* logbook, Cooke was mortally wounded by two musket balls that struck him in the chest. Quartermaster John Stewart from Berwick may have been the first seaman to go to his assistance but Cooke was already beyond help '…tell Lieutenant Cumby never to strike',[13] were his last recorded words.

Cumby assumed command at a critical moment. Four enemy ships surrounded *Bellerophon*, her main and mizzen topmasts had been shot away, damaged sails and rigging cluttered the upper decks and seamen from *L'Aigle* were preparing to board. It was probably during this phase of the battle that John Todd, a twenty-three year old able seaman from North Shields was killed at his gun and four other North East born seamen were wounded. *Bellerophon's* total casualties were high but her disciplined gunnery eventually forced *L'Aigle* to sheer away and, as she did so, *Revenge* fired two broadsides into the French ship. They had such a devastating effect that *L'Aigle* eventually surrendered to *Defiance* soon after two o'clock in the afternoon.[14]

According to the logbook of *Revenge,* Moorsom's ship entered the battle of Trafalgar at 12:40. Thereafter, 'The men [were] firing with all expedition and spirit having upon us four French ships and a Spanish three-decker'.[15]

Revenge first engaged *San Idelfonso* [74] and the French ship *Achille* [74] but was fired on by several other ships of the Combined Fleet at the same time. Moorsom's ship suffered considerable damage and sustained twenty-eight killed and fifty-one wounded during the battle. There were a number of 'Geordie' seamen amongst the casualties. William West, a twenty-three year old able seaman from Sunderland was killed; George Wilson, a quarter gunner from Newcastle and William Armour, a twenty year old able seaman pressed on Tyneside in June 1805, were both wounded. Two other seamen from the North Riding of Yorkshire, James Oburne from Whitby and William Nicholson from Scarborough were also wounded.

More than 75 per cent of the casualties sustained by the ships in Collingwood's lee column occurred on board *Royal Sovereign* and the six vessels, including *Bellerophon* and *Revenge,* that followed her into action. *Colossus,* pre-eminently the 'Geordie' ship at Trafalgar, had the dubious distinction of suffering the highest casualties of any ship in the British fleet, forty killed and 160 wounded.[16]

Colossus entered the battle about one o'clock, an hour after *Royal Sovereign* had broken through the enemy's line. She first engaged the *Swiftsure* [74], formerly a British ship captured by the French in 1801, but in the smoke and confusion *Colossus* then collided with the Spanish *Argonauta* [74]. The two ships became locked together and fought an intense gunnery duel during which both crews suffered heavy casualties. Once again the disciplined gunnery of a British ship prevailed and those of the *Argonauta* fell silent. Captain Morris was wounded during this phase of the battle but was able to remain on deck to direct operations. *Colossus* next engaged the Spanish *Bahama* [74] with her starboard guns and the French *Swiftsure* with those on the port side. Robert Jackson later recalled:

We ran the muzzles of our lower deck guns close against their side and so blazed away. Nothing was then to be heard for two hours but the thundering and cheering till at last both ships were totally dismasted and at that time the people were seen jumping off the lower gun ports of the *Bahama* Spanish seventy-four and about two minutes afterwards she struck.[17]

More than an hour after *Royal Sovereign*'s opening broadsides less than half of the ships of Nelson's fleet were engaged with French or Spanish opponents. A number of surviving accounts of this early stage of the battle describe how British ships like *Royal Sovereign*, *Bellerophon* and *Colossus* became engaged on both sides as they were surrounded by vessels of the Combined Fleet. The noise and confusion on the gun decks of these ships can hardly be imagined. George Castle, who fought at one of the heavy, 32-pounders on *Royal Sovereign*'s lower gun deck recalled, 'It was shocking to see many brave seamen mangled so, some with their heads half shot away, others with their entrails mashed lying panting upon the deck'.[18]

On board *Bellerophon* Cumby remembered:

Whilst thus closely engaged and rubbing sides with *L'Aigle* she threw many hand grenades on board of us, both on our forecastle and gangway and in at the ports, some of these exploded and dreadfully scorched some of our men...one of these grenades had been thrown in at a lower deck port and in its explosion had blown off the scuttle of the gunner's storeroom, setting fire to the storeroom and forcing open the door into the magazine passage. Most providentially...the same blast that blew open the storeroom door shut the door of the magazine, otherwise we must all in both ships have been blown up together.[19]

Victory and *Temeraire*, the leading ships in Nelson's weather column, broke through the centre of Villeneuve's line about fifteen minutes after *Royal Sovereign*. Both ships were heavily engaged on each side by French and Spanish warships. Benjamin Stevenson on *Victory* believed that '...we had seven ships upon us all at once',[20] and Louis Roteley a young lieutenant of marines was convinced that:

> A man should witness a battle in a three-decker for it beggars all description. It bewilders the sense of sight and hearing. I fancied myself in the infernal regions where every man appeared a devil.[21]

Nelson received his fatal wound about 1:15 at the height of *Victory's* duel with *Redoubtable*. Soon after Nelson was carried below Roteley, with twenty royal marines, sought to clear some of the French sharpshooters from their vantage points on *Redoubtable's* masts and rigging. He dismissed a claim, made by a French sergeant many years later, that he had been Nelson's assassin. Roteley was convinced that the individual responsible for firing the fatal shot was himself killed soon afterwards:

> The first order I gave was to clear the mizzen top when every musket was levelled at that top and in five minutes not a man was left alive in it. Some Frenchman has vaunted that he shot Nelson and survived the battle...but it must be a romance. I know the man was shot in five minutes after Nelson fell.[22]

Amongst the seamen employed to help Roteley clear *Redoubtable's* mizzen top was John King, a fifty-six year old quartermaster from Sunderland. King assisted a young midshipman by reloading his muskets with powder and ball but he was tragically killed towards the end of the encounter. King was one of three seamen from North East England killed on *Victory* at

Trafalgar, eight others were amongst the wounded. They included William Hall from Shields, aged twenty-one, an able seamen pressed at Woolwich two years before. Hall fought at *Victory's* eleventh gun and lived to tell the tale.

Another ship with strong 'Geordie' connections was *Leviathan* [74], which broke into the Combined Fleet soon after *Victory*. In passing through the enemy's line *Leviathan* fired her opening broadside into *Bucentaur,* Villeneuve's flagship, before engaging the massive Spanish four-decker, *Santissima Trinidad* [130], the largest warship in the world. *Leviathan* carried eighteen seamen from North East England into action at Trafalgar, most of them like the Master, John William Trotter, were from Tyneside. Others came from Whitby, Stockton and Berwick and some had served on the ship for a number of years. Thomas Main, for example, a thirty-nine year old quartermaster's mate from Stockton joined the ship in 1797 and Edward Lowe, an able seaman from Newcastle, had been on board since March 1798. Trotter, a relative latecomer by comparison, did not join the ship as a warrant officer until December 1803.[23] Main was a popular character with the ship's company and held a responsible position as Captain of the Forecastle. After *Leviathan* had exchanged shots with several vessels of the Combined Fleet, Captain Henry Bayntun assisted by the Master, William Trotter, was able to manoeuvre the ship into a situation of advantage relative to the Spanish ship *San Augustin.* From less than fifty yards *Leviathan* fired an accurate, double-shotted broadside into her Spanish opponent bringing down the mizzen mast and causing other serious damage. Then, by skilfully placing his ship across the bow of *San Augustin,* Bayntun was able to sweep the decks of the Spanish ship with his carronades without receiving much damage in return. After half an hour of fierce bombardment a boarding party from *Leviathan* forced the Spanish ship to surrender. *Leviathan* had four killed and twenty-two wounded. Thomas Walker a thirty-seven year old bosun's mate from Berwick and John Watson, a Master's mate from North

Seaton near Blyth, suffered burns caused by an explosion of gunpowder. James Thompson, also from Northumberland and Thomas Main from Stockton both had their left arm amputated above the elbow by the surgeon, William Shoveller, as a consequence of wounds caused by grape shot. Main's extraordinary courage in coping with the consequences of his wounds appears in almost every account of the Trafalgar battle. The story seems to have originated from a letter written by Captain Bayntun from *Leviathan* on 23 October. It began:

> I must intrude on your time by relating a trifling anecdote of one of my men, the Captain of the Forecastle, Thomas Main, who lost his arm fighting his gun. When his mates offered to take him below to the surgeon Main refused… 'I thank you, stay where you are, you will do more good there'. He made his own way to the surgeon who was prepared to treat him before others… 'Avast not till it comes to my turn, if you please', replied Main who sang the whole of Rule Britannia whilst the surgeon amputated his shattered arm below the shoulder.[24]

Sceptical, modern-day readers might point to the propaganda value of Bayntun's 'trifling anecdote' in exaggerating the bravery of British seamen and dismiss the whole story as a fairy tale. Some aspects of the story are clearly accurate and corroborated by the surgeon's journal. Whatever the truth of Main's temperament and demeanour during his ordeal, history has recorded the experience of this popular quartermaster's mate from Stockton-on-Tees.

A combination of light winds and course alterations by the Combined Fleet prevented some of the rearmost ships of Collingwood's column from reaching the battle for over three hours after *Royal Sovereign* had broken through the enemy's line. *Defence* caught up to the French *Berwick* [74] at about 2:15 and then fought *San Idelfonso* for over an hour before the Spanish ship surrendered. The much vaunted gunnery skills of *Dreadnought*'s crew were not put to the test until three o' clock in the afternoon. Collingwood's former flagship, with her main armament of ninety-eight guns, overwhelmed *San Juan Nepomuceno* which finally surrendered after half an hour of intense bombardment, with only a mainmast left standing. *Prince*, another of Collingwood's former flagships, was the last British ship to enter the battle. *Prince* was a notoriously slow sailer and, together with *Dreadnought,* had been ordered to sail a course outside Collingwood's division so as to avoid obstructing faster ships from getting into action.[25] *Prince* carried the largest number of 'Geordie' seamen after *Colossus* and *Victory,* all but one of them drafted from *Venerable* in December 1803. They were the remnants of Collingwood's 'Newcastle volunteers', and included John Watson a keelman from Dunstan. In sharp contrast to the crew of *Colossus,* *Prince* was the only ship of the line at Trafalgar without casualties at the end of the battle. A number of ships had already surrendered by the time *Prince* entered the action and others were so completely disabled that they were unable to manoeuvre or defend themselves against fresh ships. *Prince* engaged one of these ships, the French *Achille*, about 4:30, dismasted her and began a fire that quickly burned out of control. Fearing that the conflagration would spread across to his own ship, Captain Grindall ordered *Prince* to move clear and lowered boats to rescue survivors left struggling in the water. An hour later in some accounts, about 6:15 according to the logbook of *Revenge, Achille* blew up and sank.[26] An officer of *Defence* wrote:

> The hull burst into a cloud of smoke and fire. A column of vivid flame shot up into the atmosphere and terminated by expanding into a massive globe, representing for a few seconds, a prodigious tree in flames.[27]

The loss of *Achille* was a spectacular finale to the battle but few of the 'Geordies' that witnessed it were aware that Nelson died about the same time that *Prince* fired her opening broadsides at the French ship. Collingwood was told of Nelson's injuries several hours before when:

> At two thirty an officer from the *Victory* came on board and informed me of Lord Nelson being severely wounded and near expiring... [later, about 4:30]... Captain Hardy came on board and informed me of the death of the Commander in Chief.[28]

Collingwood assumed command of the British fleet with a deep sense of personal grief. He shifted his flag from *Royal Sovereign* to *Euryalus* soon afterwards 'that I might the better distribute my orders'.[29] Officially, Trafalgar cost the lives of 449 British officers, seamen and marines. A further 1214 were listed as wounded many of whom died during the days and weeks that followed. Losses amongst soldiers and seamen of the Combined Fleet are not certainly known but some estimates place the number of French dead at 2000 and those in the Spanish ships at about half that number. Over 11,000 prisoners were taken, many of them wounded.[30] As the guns fell silent after more than five hours of fighting, the surviving seamen set about the task of making temporary repairs to damaged hulls, masts and rigging and taking their prizes in tow. In the relief and exhaustion of victory few could have imagined that a new ordeal was about to begin.

References

1.   Lavery, *Nelson's* Fleet, pp. 140-141.

2.   The Cumby Letter – *An account of the proceedings of H.M. ship* Bellerophon *in the battle of Trafalgar*, The Nelson Dispatch, vol. 6, part 6 (April 1998), p. 237.

3.   Clayton, T. and Craig, P. *Trafalgar, the men, the battle, the storm*, Hodder and Stoughton (London, 2004), p. 114.

4.   Extract of a letter from Robert Jackson of South Shields to his parents, *Newcastle Courant*, 21 December 1805, p. 2, col. 2.

5.   The Cumby Letter, p. 238.

6.   Lavery, *Nelson's Fleet*, p. 149 citing NMM LBK/38 and the muster book of *Bellerophon*, NA, ADM 36/16498.

7.   Admiral Collingwood's Journals, May 1805 – September 1806, NA, ADM 50/41.

8.   The Jackson Letter, *Newcastle Courant*, 21 December 1805.

9.   Admiral Collingwood's Journals, NA, ADM 50/41.

10.   Clayton and Craig, *Trafalgar*, p. 156.

11.   Lavery, *Nelson's Fleet*, p. 159.

12.   George Castle's Trafalgar Letter, *Nelson Dispatch*, vol. 6, part 8 (October 1998), p. 346.

13.   Cordingly, *Billy Ruffian*, p. 195.

14.   Cordingly, *Billy Ruffian*, p. 198.

15.   Logbook of *Revenge*, NA, ADM 51/1535.

16.   See, http://www.genuki.org.uk//big/eng/Trafalgar/Ships.txt.

17.   The Jackson Letter, *Newcastle Courant*, 21 December 1805.

18.   The Castle Letter, *Nelson Dispatch*, p. 346.

19. The Cumby Letter, p. 243.

20. Benjamin Stevenson to his sister in Gateshead, written from *Victory*, 5 November 1805. Ayshford Complete Trafalgar Roll.

21. Lavery, *Nelson's Fleet*, p. 165.

22. Clayton and Craig, *Trafalgar*, p. 205.

23. Muster book of *Leviathan*, NA, ADM 36/15837.

24. Extract of a letter from Captain Bayntun of *Leviathan* off Cape Trafalgar, 23 October 1805, *Newcastle Courant*, 14 December 1805, p. 2, col. 2.

25. Clayton and Craig, *Trafalgar*, p. 135.

26. Logbook of *Revenge*, NA, ADM 50/1535.

27. Clayton and Craig, *Trafalgar*, p. 251.

28. Admiral Collingwood's Journals, NA, ADM 50/41.

29. Newnham-Collingwood, *Correspondence of Lord Collingwood*, p. 137.

30. Clayton and Craig, *Trafalgar*, p. 252.

*'I am left safe and unhurt both from the Enemy and the Elements, for
I can safely say we have engaged both...'*

[George Castle, *H.M.S. Royal Sovereign,*
Gibraltar, 3 November 1805]

After Trafalgar

Nelson intended to anchor his fleet at the end of the battle.
His final signal from *Victory,* 'Prepare to anchor after close of day',
was acknowledged by officers of several ships including Cumby
on *Bellerophon.* Collingwood's decision not to do so has been a
source of controversy ever since. Edward Codrington, captain of
Orion, was the most prominent of several contemporary critics of
Collingwood's indecision and failure to anchor during the evening
after the battle. Codrington argued that anchoring immediately
would have enabled the British ships to regroup, repair what
damage they could and secure all seventeen of the enemy's ships
taken as prizes. Collingwood's defenders take the view that the
Admiral's judgement was influenced by the shattered condition
of some of his ships, many of them without masts or the means
to manouevre, and the presence of dangerous shoals on a lee shore.
Collingwood himself never explained a rationale for his decision
although sheer fatigue seems to have played a part in it. He probably
hoped to gain some distance from the land during the hours of
darkness, very much a sailor's instinct, but wind and weather soon

intervened. The barometer fell sharply during the night and the wind increased to a fresh breeze from the south. By mid-afternoon on 22 October it was blowing a full gale with gusts of over fifty miles per hour accompanied by driving rain. In these circumstances, so close inshore, Collingwood's ships struggled to preserve themselves as well as their prizes. Hundreds of British seamen had been placed as prize crews on warships captured during the battle but deteriorating weather conditions jeopardised their chances of being taken off again.

The first ship to be lost was *Fougueux*, the same vessel that fired on *Royal Sovereign* in the opening minutes of the battle. By the evening of 21 October she had become a dismasted and waterlogged hulk. A prize crew of British seamen, most of them from *Temeraire*, fought a losing battle to keep *Fougueux* afloat but were eventually forced to admit defeat. Boats lowered from the frigate *Phoebe* rescued dozens of seamen but darkness and rough seas made it difficult to continue and many others were left on board. *Fougueux* was driven aground and wrecked the following day with the loss of almost everyone on board. Less than two days after surviving the shot and musketry of Trafalgar, twenty-four seamen from *Temeraire* were amongst those who were drowned. They included William Featherstonehaugh, aged forty-nine, a quartermaster from Sunderland. Featherstonehaugh had joined *Temeraire* from the frigate *Andromache* (32) in February 1804 as a volunteer together with four other 'Geordies' and a seaman from Whitby. Two of the 'Geordies', both of them from Newcastle, were wounded at Trafalgar. Richard Hugh, an able seaman from Stockton, was killed.[1]

On 22 October as conditions worsened in Cadiz Bay, Collingwood's fleet lost control of several more prizes including *L'Aigle*, damaged and dismasted by *Bellerophon*'s gunfire during the battle and, *Redoubtable*, the ship responsible for Nelson's demise. *L'Aigle*, navigated by surviving members of the crew and fifty seamen from *Defiance*, managed to anchor close inshore. *Redoubtable*, which was further out to sea with a prize crew from *Swiftsure* on board, seemed to be making some progress until she lost her only standing mast in the rising gale. Without sails to keep her steady, *Redoubtable* rolled deeply in the heavy seas and began to ship more water than the pumps could handle. The prize master, Lieutenant Thomas Read, decided to abandon ship and made a distress signal to *Swiftsure*. Five boats were lowered into mountainous seas and fought their way to the wreck. In repeated journeys during the hours that followed they succeeded in rescuing more than two hundred men. It was perhaps the most heroic episode of the Trafalgar storm. *Redoubtable*'s stern was already under water when the last boats left and she sank during the night with hundreds of men still on board. Some were rescued the following day but five seamen from *Swiftsure* and twelve from *Temeraire* were drowned in the wreck. John Smith, an able seaman from Newcastle, who had served on *Swiftsure* for a year, was the second man from the region to be lost on a prize. Smith was one of thirteen seamen from North East England who served on *Swiftsure* at Trafalgar. Two of them, Edward Davidson from North Shields and Roger Liddle from Sunderland, lived long enough to claim their Trafalgar medals and tell the tale to their grandchildren. Other seamen from the region, four on *Defence* and three on *Dreadnought*, helped to navigate two of the captured prizes into Gibraltar in early November.[2]

The Trafalgar storm reached its greatest intensity between 26 and 28 October when, using modern meteorological descriptions, the strength of the wind reached Storm Force Ten gusting to Violent Storm Eleven with persistent driving rain. Most of the remaining prizes were lost, recaptured or deliberately sunk during this time. The only ship to avoid the worst of the storm was *Belleisle*, the first ship to arrive at Gibraltar, towed in by the frigate *Naiad* on 24 October. Seven ships arrived the following Sunday including *Revenge*, *Colossus* towed in by *Agamemnon*, *Bellerophon* and *Victory. Royal Sovereign* with *Temeraire* did not arrive until 3 November. Soon after his arrival at Gibraltar, George Castle sat down to write his account of the battle. It began:

> By the great mercy of God I am left safe and unhurt from the Enemy and the Elements for I can safely say we have engaged both, but thank God our poor shattered ship has arrived here this evening after tossing about more than a week at the mercy of wind and waves...[3]

Castle's fellow midshipman on *Royal Sovereign*, Grenville Thompson, was less fortunate. Thompson was severely wounded in the left arm by grapeshot and suffered a splinter wound that had broken his leg.[4] He was admitted to Gibraltar hospital with numerous other seamen, many of whom subsequently died of their wounds. At least four men from North East England are recorded to have died at Gibraltar, amongst them Thomas Main the popular seaman of *Leviathan*. Main had survived the amputation of his left arm during the battle and seemed to be on the road to recovery, but he became feverish and died on 15 November a few days after the ship arrived at Gibraltar.[5]

Amongst the first ships to leave for England in company with *Victory* were *Belleisle* and *Bellerophon*. They sailed on 5 November and took a month to reach Plymouth. *Bellerophon's* captain was now Edward Rotheram whom Collingwood had transferred from *Royal Sovereign* on 4 November. What Cumby thought of his new captain is unrecorded although it is clear that Rotheram recognised and respected the abilities of his first lieutenant. When *Bellerophon* arrived at Plymouth in December Rotheram responded to the Admiralty's request for him to recommend officers he considered worthy of promotion. On 17 December Rotheram replied:

I have received your letter of 14th informing me of their Lordships' intentions to promote the first lieutenants of the line of battle ships lately under the command of Vice-Admiral Lord Nelson in the action of 21 October last providing their conduct has merited the approbation of their respective captains and directing me to make my report... In answer to which I have to acquaint you that Lieutenant Pryce Cumby was first lieutenant of the *Bellerophon* the whole of the action of 21 October, that he fought the ship sometime after the captain was slain and I am well persuaded will merit any favour their Lordships' may be pleased to bestow on him.[6]

Cumby was promoted captain in January 1806 and together with Rotheram attended Nelson's funeral. Collingwood's former lieutenant on *Dreadnought*, William Landless, was passed over in the round of Trafalgar promotions despite the Admiral's letters of recommendation on his behalf. In March-April 1806 Collingwood wrote two long and agitated letters to Lord Barham from *Queen* expressing his irritation that the Admiralty had failed to promote Landless after Trafalgar:

I can now say what will scarcely be credited and what I am willing to believe your Lordship is not aware of that I am the only commander in that fleet who has not had, by the courtesy of the Admiralty, an opportunity to advance an officer of any description. Lieutenant Landless, the only person I recommended to your Lordship, is an old and valuable officer who has followed me from ship to ship the whole of the war and I did hope that my earnest recommendation might have gained him favour.

I cannot help thinking that there must be something
in my conduct in which your Lordship did not
approve... by denying to my dependents and friends
what is so liberally given to other ships in the fleet.[7]

The justice of Collingwood's complaints were eventually
recognised and Landless was promoted commander in August
1806. He later achieved the rank of captain and died at Easington,
near Belford, in 1827. Another Northumberland-born officer,
James Lilburne, who served as first lieutenant of *Swiftsure* at
Trafalgar and was promoted captain in April 1806, did not live to
enjoy retirement. He was killed in action at Malaga in April 1812
when in command of *Goshawk*.

Collingwood never returned to his native Northumberland
after Trafalgar. He was showered with honours, ennobled by
George III, given a pension of £2000 per year and promoted
commander in chief of the British Mediterranean Fleet. Always
courteous, diligent and diplomatic with a strong sense of his public
duty, Collingwood became so totally absorbed in the
responsibilities of his position that he literally worked himself to
death. He became a remote and rather melancholy figure with
only his famous dog Bounce to keep him company. Soon after
shifting from *Queen* to a new flagship *Ville de Paris* in April 1809,
Collingwood wrote to his sister from Port Mahon in Minorca:

Tough as I am I cannot last much longer. I have seen all
the ships and men out two or three times. Bounce and
I seem to be the only personages that stand our ground.[8]

Bounce fell overboard and drowned in August 1809.
Collingwood grew weaker as his medical condition, probably cancer
of the stomach, steadily worsened. He sent his letter of resignation
to Lord Mulgrave at the Admiralty in February 1810 declaring

that he was no longer capable of performing his duty. He died at sea on board *Ville de Paris* two days out from Minorca, on her passage back to England on 7 March 1810. Collingwood's young midshipmen, Grenville Thompson and George Castle were subsequently promoted lieutenant, Thompson in 1809 and Castle in 1811. As followers of Collingwood however, the Admiral's death deprived them of influence and would certainly have had a detrimental effect on their prospects of further promotion. Thompson was still a lieutenant when he died of fever in the West Indies in February 1818. George Castle died in 1827. Access to influence at the Admiralty was never a problem for Constantine Moorsom. After Trafalgar his father, Robert, moved into naval administration becoming an Admiralty Commissioner in 1809 and Surveyor General of the Ordnance between 1810 and 1820. Constantine Moorsom was promoted lieutenant in 1812 and became a post-captain in 1818 at the age of twenty-six. He later became the Chairman of the London and North Western Railway and died a Vice-Admiral in London in 1861.

William Cumby was in the West Indies when Collingwood died. He had been appointed to command *Polyphemus* in May 1808 and sailed out to the Caribbean where he served under Admiral Rowley. In June 1809 Cumby distinguished himself once again in command of a squadron sent from Port Royal, Jamaica, to capture Santo Domingo. A number of Trafalgar 'Geordies' who remained on board *Polyphemus* took part in that operation. One of them, John Foster, a thirty-four year old royal marine from Gosforth who joined the ship in 1804, may well have been wounded during the fighting. Foster died on board *Polyphemus* in September 1809.[9] In 1811 Cumby was appointed to *Hyperion* [36] a frigate that he commanded in North American and Canadian waters until the end of the Napoleonic War. As captain of *Hyperion* Cumby represented a new breed of naval officer concerned for the welfare of his men and progressive in his attitude towards the training of young officers under his command. Midshipmen of *Hyperion*, for example, were obliged to submit their personal, navigational journals to Captain Cumby every day '…as soon as maybe after noon', and were to be '…sent aloft at daybreak and nightfall to look around the horizon'.[10] Discipline and routine were strictly maintained but Cumby prohibited petty officers of *Hyperion* from indulging in an age old, but much resented, practice known as 'starting'. It was common in the navy for boatswain's mates to carry a knotted rattan or rope's end which they frequently used on the backs and shoulders of seamen as a way of 'encouraging' them to their duties. Cumby considered it a 'highly improper practice', and told his petty officers that it was 'most peremtorily (sic) forbidden'.[11]

Cumby retired from active service on 31 August 1815. As a frigate captain, Cumby accumulated considerable sums of prize money which he used to construct Trafalgar House at Heighington in County Durham, where he lived for most of his retirement. William Pryce Cumby died in September 1837 soon after his appointment as Superintendent of Pembroke Dock. He lies buried in South Wales but there is an elaborate commemorative plaque to him in St. Michael's Parish Church, Heighington.[12]

Edward Rotheram had a less successful career. He remained in command of *Bellerophon* until June 1808 although his temperament and manner continued to irritate many of the officers who came into contact with him. In October 1806 he was reprimanded by Admiral St. Vincent who alleged that Rotheram's negligence and lack of seamanship had been responsible for the loss of *Bellerophon*'s topmasts in a gale off Ushant. St. Vincent insisted that the cost of repairs should be deducted from Rotheram's wages. He was in trouble with the Admiralty again the following year for 'un-officer like conduct' towards the chaplain and junior officers of *Bellerophon*. When Collingwood came to hear of Rotheram's misfortunes he wrote from *Ocean*:

I am sorry to hear of poor Rotheram, though I think
him a stupid man, I was in hope that he would have
gone on in the ship I put him in which I believe was
the only chance of being in a ship.[13]

In view of Rotheram's cantankerous nature and his limited
abilities as a sea officer it seems ironic that he left such a valuable
legacy to naval historians of the Nelson era. As captain of
Bellerophon, Rotheram compiled a remarkably detailed survey of
seamen in the ship's company. It represents, according to one naval
historian:

A unique picture of the composition, background and
outward appearance of the crew of a British ship of the
line in the years following Trafalgar.[14]

Rotheram's survey offers biographical detail about 387 men.
Almost half of them were English born and 45 per cent of
Bellerophon's crew had been merchant seamen prior to their service
in the navy. Many of these men had been victims of the press
gang.[15]

Collingwood's prediction that Rotheram was unlikely to
achieve a further command proved to be correct. The Admiralty
overlooked him after he left *Bellerophon* in 1808 and he had no
further service at sea. After the war Rotheram complained that he
had not been included amongst the Trafalgar captains created
Knight Commander of the Bath, and was given the lesser honour
of Companion of the Bath. Thereafter, he continued to make a
nuisance of himself writing critical letters to national newspapers
about various aspects of naval policy with which he did not agree:

About the organisation of the Navy Board to *The Times*
in 1817; the ennobling of certain mediocre naval
officers to the *Morning Chronicle* in 1825; the fast

promotion given to certain members of the Melville family to the *Morning Herald* in 1826; and the state of the naval administration to the *Sun* in the same year.[16]

In 1825, when it was announced that *Royal Sovereign* was to be taken into dock for the purpose of being reduced to a prison hulk, Rotheram requested and was presented with several substantial pieces of timber taken from the quarterdeck and quarterdeck beams of the ship, 'where that officer chiefly remained during the battle of Trafalgar'. He then had them made into a piece of furniture.[17]

Rotheram was appointed Captain of Greenwich Hospital in 1828 and died at Bildeston in Suffolk, in 1830.

Most naval officers like Rotheram were able to live in comfortable retirement at the end of their naval careers. Post-war life was very different for the majority of seamen released from naval service in 1815. For many of them the Napoleonic War ended as the French Revolutionary War had begun, with strikes and trade disputes about wages and conditions in the coal trade. A combination of over-capacity in the shipping industry and a temporary surplus of maritime labour in the ports of North East England restricted seamen's opportunities for employment. The situation was exacerbated by shipowners who sought to reduce wages and restrict manning levels for a voyage in the coal trade. Once again the discipline and organised solidarity of merchant seamen on the Tyne and Wear resisted these innovations and the resultant strike stopped the coal trade for more than six weeks during September-October 1815.[18] Despite these early setbacks the expansion of the coal trade during the years that followed provided regular and remunerative employment for many of the seamen pressed into the Royal Navy during the French Wars. In 1830, as the steam age gathered pace and demand for coal grew, there were over ten thousand voyages in the coal trade from the ports of North East England.[19]

Returning keelmen also struggled to adjust to post-war conditions. Technological change, particularly the expansion of colliery waggonways worked by steam locomotives, the employment of steam tugs and the increasing use of coal 'spouts' as a means of delivering coal directly into the holds of waiting colliers, threatened employment opportunities for keelmen, particularly those who worked the river Tyne 'below bridge'. Two keelmen's strikes in 1819 and 1822, as well as protracted litigation during the 1820s challenging the legality of the coal 'spouts', failed to win them any concessions. Nevertheless, despite these threats to their livelihood, the keelmen continued to make an important contribution to the expansion of the coal trade. In Whickham Parish in 1835, keelmen still represented the largest single occupational group amongst heads of families and their traditional communities at Swalwell and Dunstan survived well into the 1840s.[20] However, by this date, only a handful of survivors of the 'vast body of fine men' pressed by Mackenzie in 1803 continued to live there.[21] Nicholas Beales from Dunstan and William Gardner from Blaydon, who served on *Colossus*, together with John Watson of *Prince*, were alive to claim their Trafalgar medals in 1848. There may have been other keelmen amongst twenty-five Trafalgar veterans from North East England who lived to claim their medals.[22]

Few of these seamen left any permanent record of their naval service. George Irwin, the seaman from Hexham whose *Voyages and Adventures* was first published in 1830, seems to be the only account written from the perspective of a North Country seaman on the lower deck. William Richardson's *A Mariner of England* is better known but most of it was written from the perspective of a naval warrant officer. Unfortunately, neither one of these seamen fought at Trafalgar.[23] However, a rare survival that does offer biographical information for the naval service of some 'Trafalgar Geordies' are two annual reports (those for 1843 and 1844) of the Tyne Aged Sailors and Scullermen's Society. The Society owned fourteen small rowing boats which it leased to aged mariners at six pence per week. The boats were used to ferry passengers across the river and enabled the old men to earn a modest income. Almost all of the old seamen entitled to use the Society's boats were over sixty years of age and had served in the Royal Navy as young men. Boat number five, for example, was leased to James Donnison aged sixty-eight, who spent fifty years at sea. Donnison was first impressed in 1793 and served on *Agamemnon* under Nelson in 1795. Boat number eleven was leased by William Sim aged sixty-three. Sim had been impressed in 1799 and subsequently received ten pounds from the Patriotic Fund as compensation for the wounds he received on *Orion* at the battle of Trafalgar. John Stranger aged sixty-eight had been impressed in 1804 and was, according to the description in the Annual Report, '...at the battle of Trafalgar but not in action'. In 1843 after forty-five years at sea Stranger was forced to retire:

> Having got a perishment of cold when shipwrecked which has affected him with rheumatism to such a degree as to render him unfit for service.[24]

Many of these men must have witnessed the dedication of the Collingwood Monument at Tynemouth in 1845.

Thomas Haswell's account of North Shields in the mid-nineteenth century contains a number of references to:

> The sea-dogs of Camperdown, of the Nile, of Trafalgar. Scores were to be found on the quays, the wharves, the landing places and lower streets of old Shields, in every stage of picturesque dismemberment – one arm, one

The *Defence* at the Battle of the First of June, 1794 *by Nicholas Pocock 1811*
Defence, centre, was the first ship into action, suffered severe damage and was totally dismasted. *Defence* was involved in the Spithead Mutiny in 1797 and fought at the Battle of the Nile 1798. Twenty-seven North Country seamen served on *Defence* at Trafalgar. *National Maritime Museum, London.*

Situation of the *Colossus* when closely engaged by *Bahama*, Spanish 74 and *Swiftsure*, French 74, *by Jonathan Needham (Engraver). Colossus carried more 'North Country' seamen than any other ship at Trafalgar. She also suffered the highest number of casualties. National Maritime Museum, London.*

Bounty Paid	N°	Entry	Year	Appearance	Whence and whether Preft or aot.	Place and County where Born	Age a Time of Entry "this Ship	N° and Letter of Tickets	MENS NAMES	Qualites	D. D.D. or R	Time of Discharge
	436	Nov 1814	Nov 1	J.B		Trenant	22		Tho⁵ Danlop	Ord		
		"	"	"		Gladmore	28		Wm Duncan	Ord		
		"	"	"		Stonehive	38		Wm Robinson	Ord		
	440	"	"	"		Leith	20		Geo Robinson	Ord		
	442	"	"	"		Glasgow	22		Davd Bryson	Ord		
		"	"	"		Paisley	27		Alexr Dove	Ord		
		"	"	"		Greenock	20		Archd McLachlan	Ord		
	445	"	"	"		Paisley	22		Alexr Stark	Ord		
	446	"	"	"		Edinbro	25		Thos Arnott	carps mate		
		"	"	"		Isle of Sey	20		Neil McInnes	Ord		
		"	"	"		S. Shields	20		Ralph Fellock	Ord		
	451	"	"	"		Ousburn Newcastle	20		Wm Surtees	Ord		
		"	"	"		Newcastle	20		Henr Barron	Ord		
		"	"	"		Long Benton Newcastle	20		Wm Anderson	Ord	DD 23 Oct	
	455	"	"	"		Blaydon	20		Peter Legg	Ab		
		"	"	"		Do	25		Wm Gardner	Ab		
		"	"	"		Lynn Norfolk	22		Geo Moffatt	Ord		
		"	"	"		Newcastle	35		Math McWinship	Ord		
		"	"	"		Dunsell Newcastle	20		Richd Maddison	Ord		
	460	"	"	"		Newcastle	35		Geo Simpson	Ord		

Muster book of Colossus

A page from the muster book of *Colossus* records the names of some of the Keelmen pressed on Tyneside in 1803. Wm. Anderson from Long Benton was DD [Discharged Dead] two days after the battle but William Gardner from Blaydon lived to claim his Trafalgar medal in 1848.

The National Archives (PRO): ref. ADM36/15825

Vice-Admiral Lord Collingwood (1748-1810) *by William Owen.*
'A better seaman, a better friend to seamen, never trod a quarterdeck.' (Robert Hay)
Tyne & Wear Museums.

Lieutenant Grenville Thompson (1788-1818)
One of Collingwood's midshipmen, Thompson was severely wounded on *Royal Sovereign* at Trafalgar.
He died of fever in the West Indies in 1818.
Tyne & Wear Museums.

Edward Rotherham (1753-1830) *Robert Pollard*
'I have a gentleman from Newcastle as my captain but he is a man of no talent as a sea officer and of very little assistance to me.' (Admiral Collingwood)
National Maritime Museum, London.

William Pryce Cumby (1771-1837)
'Lieutenant Pryce Cumby was First Lieutenant of *Bellerophon* the whole of the action of 21 October … and I am well persuaded will merit any favour their Lordships may be pleased to bestow on him'. (Captain Edward Rotheram) *Private Collection.*

Situation of H.M. Ship Bellerophon, by Joy Williamson (Artist).
Bellerophon, third from the right engaged between *L'Aigle* and *Monarca* about the time Captain Cooke was killed.
National Maritime Museum, London.

Men o' War off Portsmouth *J.W. Carmichael* c. 1848

A lively scene at the entrance to Portsmouth harbour in the final decade of sailing warships. A frigate (left) and a naval cutter (right) prepare to enter harbour as a ship of the line (centre) heels before a favourable breeze and heads for the open sea. *Tyne & Wear Museums.*

leg, one arm and one leg... grimly suggestive of the
peculiar horror of 'tween deck fighting.

Haswell even named some of them:

Jack Crutwell of the *Bellerophon*; John Hunter too,
who'd been with Nelson; Gideon Dodgin of the
Amethyst and *Metis*; William Hall, eleventh gun on
the *Victory*... hardy, patient long-suffering fellows,
whose bronzed faces spoke in every line of hardship
and privation. Cheery and good-naturedly responsive
when addressed, but mostly reflective, taciturn and
observant.[25]

Sir Walter Runciman, another contemporary observer of the
merchant seamen of North East England recalled some of the
characters of his childhood in his autobiographical *Before the Mast
- And After*:

I think it was in the winter of 1855 that three old sailors
came on a visit...one was my grandfather and the other
two were my great-uncles. All three had been in the
navy and had fought together in many sea battles,
notably at Copenhagen, the Nile and Trafalgar. Their
conversation was a joy when they could be induced to
relate their experiences of their conflicts with French
and Spanish battleships...thrills never to be forgotten
by youthful listeners.[26]

Old age and infirmity gradually took its toll on these old
mariners and many 'Trafalgar Geordies' ended their days on poor
relief. Wounded and disabled seamen were entitled to receive a
small annual pension from the Greenwich Hospital fund, a few
lived in the hospital itself as Greenwich Pensioners, but the

Victorian workhouse became the final residence of those unable to support themselves on outdoor relief. In 1860 there were 1149 former naval seamen receiving poor relief in England and Wales, over fifty of them resident in North East England. Poor Law Guardians at Tynemouth and Sunderland were responsible for most of these old men and at least two of them were Trafalgar veterans. William Sim of Tynemouth, then aged eighty-one, who served on *Orion* and Roger Liddle, aged eighty-four, from Sunderland who had been an able seaman on *Swiftsure* were receiving outdoor relief in 1860.[27]

Liddle served fourteen years in the Royal Navy during the French Wars and together with Sim they were amongst the oldest surviving witness of Trafalgar still living in North East England. Two former midshipmen, both of them wounded during the battle, laid claim to being the last North Country seamen to have fought at Trafalgar. George Galloway from Guisborough, who served as a fourteen-year old on *Thunderer*, died in 1873. George Wharrie, who was living at West Hartlepool in 1872, was almost certainly the last of them. He died in Liverpool on 2 August 1875 at the age of eighty-eight. Wharrie served on *Colossus* at Trafalgar, the ship that carried the largest number of 'Geordie' sailors and suffered the highest casualties of any ship in Nelson's fleet that day.

References

1. They were Thomas Glendenning, Yeoman of the Sheets, aged 51 and William Gordon, an able seaman, aged 37. Gordon received a lacerated wound to the left ankle and was invalided from the navy in 1806. Detail derived from Ayshford Complete Trafalgar Roll.

2. Clayton and Craig, *Trafalgar*, pp. 282-284 and Ayshford Complete Trafalgar Roll.

3.   The Castle Letter, *Nelson Dispatch*, p. 346.

4.   *Newcastle Courant*, 23 November 1805, p. 2 col. 4.

5.   A list of all the casualties suffered by men from North East England can be found in Appendix Two.

6.   NA, ADM 1/2408.

7.   Admiral Collingwood to Lord Barham, 28 March 1806, Newnham-Collingwood, *Correspondence of Lord Collingwood*, pp. 201-202.

8.   Klukvin, *Collingwood*, p. 34.

9.   Muster book of *Polyphemus*, Ayshford Complete Trafalgar Roll.

10. Lavery, *Nelson's Navy*, p. 90 and p. 200.

11. Lavery, *Nelson's Navy*, p. 219.

12. Dean, G. & Evans, K. *Nelson's Heroes*, The Nelson Society (1994), p. 58-59.

13. Staniforth, *Collingwood and Rotheram*, p. 15.

14. Cordingly, *Billy Ruffian*, p. 209.

15. Cordingly, *Billy Ruffian*, pp. 210-212.

16. Lavery, *Nelson's Fleet*, p. 198.

17. *Newcastle Courant*, 23 July 1825, p. 4 col. 3.

18. McCord, N. *The Seamen's Strike of 1815 in North East England*, Economic History Review, XXI (Second Series), 1968, pp. 127-143.

19. Flinn, M.W. *The History of the British Coal Industry*, vol. 2, (Oxford University Press, 1984), p. 172.

20. Rowe, D.J. *The Decline of the Tyneside Keelmen in the Nineteenth Century*, Northern History, vol. VI (1969), pp. 111-131.

21. McCord, *Impress Service*, p. 25.

22. The names and details of these seamen are listed in Appendix 3.

23. Irwin, G. *Narrative of the Voyages and Adventures of George Irwin* (Hexham 1830). Richardson, W. *A Mariner of England*, first edition 1907, reprinted by Conway Maritime Press (1970). The best-known account of the battle of Trafalgar from the perspective of a seaman on the lower deck, *Jack Nastyface: Memoirs of a Seaman* was first published in 1836. It was written by William Robinson who served under Captain Moorsom of *Revenge*.

24. Annual Reports of the Tyne Aged Sailors and Scullermen's Society, 1843 and 1844. TWAS

25. Haswell, *The Maister*, p. 132.

26. Runciman, Sir W. *Before the Mast – And After*, Fisher and Unwin (London, 1924). pp. 19-20.

27. Bell, G. *Royal Navy seamen receiving poor relief – February 1860*, Microfiche summary derived from The Report of the Royal Commission on the Internal Economy and Management of the Greenwich Hospital, Parliamentary Papers 1860 (2678) XXXI.

Map1

Royal Sovereign opens fire

'About noon the Royal Sovereign *opened a fire on the 12, 13, 14 and 15 ships from the enemy's rear, and stood on with all sail for the enemy's line.'*

[Admiral Collingwood's Journal]

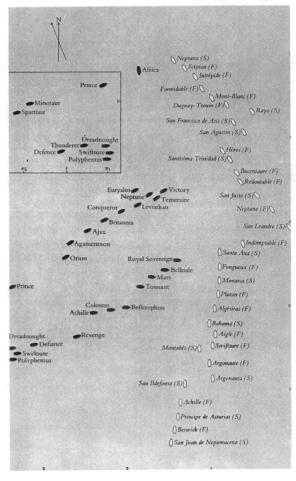

Map 2

Victory and Temeraire break the line

> '*A man should witness a battle on a three-decker for it beggars all description... I fancied myself in the infernal regions where every man appeared a devil.*'
>
> [Lieutenant Louis Roteley, Royal Marines, *H.M.S. Victory*]

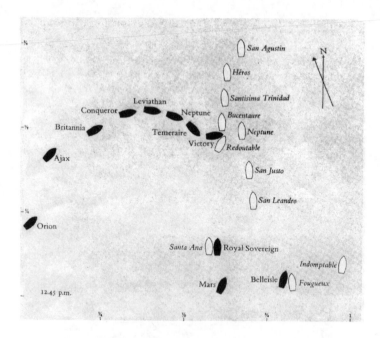

Map 3

Bellerophon and Colossus closely engaged
'*We ran in between two of them so close the muzzles of our lower deck guns were close against their side and so blazed away.*'

[Robert Jackson of South Shields, Able Seaman, *H.M.S. Colossus*]

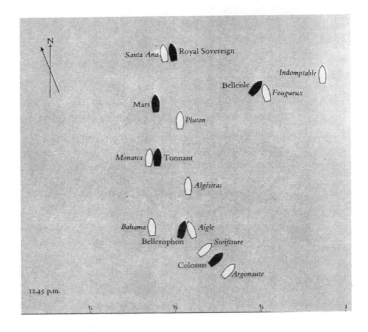

Appendix One

Muster Books of Selected Warships

Seamen from all over North East England served in varying numbers on every ship that fought at the battle of Trafalgar. Their names, age and positions on board, the date of their first appearance on the ship and whether or not they had volunteered or were impressed, can be found in the muster books at the National Archives, Kew, listed under ADM 36 and 37. The author has researched the muster books of each of the warships listed in the Appendix, with the exception of *Prince*. The latter is derived from the Ayshford Complete Trafalgar Roll. This is a fascinating and thoroughly researched source of information about the men who fought at Trafalgar and is highly recommended to genealogists and family historians who wish to establish whether an ancestor fought at the battle. Ayshford Complete Trafalgar Roll is published by Pam and Derek Ayshford, SEFF, 544 rue Vanderkindere, B-1180, Brussels.

The abbreviations used in the tables are as follows:

LM Landsman; OS Ordinary Seaman; AB Able Seaman; YS Yeoman of the Sheets; QM Quartermaster; QMM Quartermaster's Mate; Mid Midshipman; MM Master's Mate; BM Boatswain's Mate; YPR Yeoman of the Powder Room.

Bellerophon

Name	Age	Born	Position
William Ferguson	33	Shields	Quarter Gunner
Henry Park	23	Whitby	YS
Michael Todd	26	Sunderland	YS
John Todd	23	Shields	AB
John Burton	26	Berwick	OS
John Green	29	Newcastle	Carpenter's Mate
Edward Ford	22	Sunderland	OS
Jonathan Eddison	21	Berwick	AB
Richard Nicholson	34	Blyth, Northumberland	Carpenter's Crew
John Stewart	36	Berwick	QM
John Fox	27	Whitby	AB
James Brown	25	Whitby	AB
Thomas Taylor	32	Newcastle	AB
Henry Freeman	36	Newcastle	Quarter Gunner

Source: NA ADM 36/16498

Colossus

Name	Age	Born	Position
Luke Anderson	33	Newcastle	MM
John Bells	26	Durham	LM
Thomas Goodrich	26	Durham	Carpenter's Mate
Hardin Hall	45	Sunderland	QM
Robert Jackson	21	South Shields	AB
Benjamin Hopper	30	Etal, Northumberland	AB
Jonathan Featherstone	31	Whitby	QM
James Macgregor	20	Newcastle	AB
George Rule	20	Newcastle	AB
Alexander Thompson	25	Berwick	LM
Thomas Banks	28	North Shields	AB
Jonathan James	50	North Shields	AB
Joshua Pollard	20	Stockton	AB
William Jackson	24	Newcastle	AB
John Jackson	20	Sunderland	AB
Miles M Ward	25	Newcastle	AB
Thomas Lindsay	24	South Shields	AB
Henry Lindsay	20	South Shields	AB
Thomas Moore	20	South Shields	AB
William Venus	22	North Shields	AB
Jacob Venus	20	North Shields	AB
George Rutherford	43	Newcastle	AB
Jacob Cairns	27	Newcastle	AB
William Taylor	20	Newcastle	AB
Samuel Somerville	20	Durham	AB
Thomas Leek	27	Blaydon	AB
Robert Robinson	27	Newcastle	AB
Robert Foster	38	Newcastle	AB

continued

Colossus

Name	Age	Born	Position
Thomas Howey	29	North Shields	AB
Charles Matthews	30	Whitby	Carpenter's Crew
James Guthrie	23	Blaydon	OS
Sunley Milburn	20	Whitby	LM
John Fowler	35	Newcastle	Caulker's mate
Ralph Tullock	20	South Shields	OS
Henry Barron	20	Newcastle	OS
William Surtees	20	Newcastle	OS
William Anderson	20	Longbenton	AB
Peter Legg	20	Blaydon	AB
Wm Gardner	25	Blaydon	OS
Matthew Winship	25	Newcastle	OS
Richard Maddison	20	Dunston	OS
George Simpson	35	Newcastle	OS
John Lambert	20	Newcastle	OS
Jonathan Purdue	20	Newcastle	OS
Mark Liddle	20	Newcastle	OS
James Ewart	27	Newcastle	Armourer's Mate
James Christie	20	Newcastle	OS
Jonathan Brown	20	Swalwell	OS
Jonathan Hedley	22	Howdonpans	Ship's Corporal
William J Masterman	35	Pickering	Mid
Henry Dunn	26	North Shields	AB
Nicholas Beales	24	Dunston	AB
Robert Walker	29	Shields	QM
Robert Wilson	24	Durham	AB
George Trewhitt	21	Shields	AB
Matthew Swan	19	North Shields	AB
Rowlandson Maclean	20	Berwick	Mid

Source: NA ADM 36/15825

Leviathan

Name	Age	Born	Position
John Wright	30	Newcastle	Sergeant, Royal Marines.
William Anderson	40	Stockton	Mid.
Thomas Main	39	Stockton	QMM
Henry Dobinson	28	South Shields	AB
Edward Lowe	24	Newcastle	AB
Robert Lindsey	43	South Shields	AB
John Ayres	22	Durham	AB
James Baker	23	Whitby	OS
James Thompson	33	Jarrow	AB
Thomas Smith	27	Northumberland	AB
George Fall	43	Sunderland	BM
John Watson	27	Northumberland	MM
John William Trotter	37	Gateshead	Master
John Yellaly	22	Newcastle	LM
James Blake	17	Newcastle	LM
Richard Hunter	43	Whitby	Carpenter's crew
James Courby	26	Newcastle	AB
Thomas Walker	37	Berwick	BM

Source: NA ADM 36/15837

Prince

Name	Age	Place	Position
James Bilby	20	Shields	OS
James Bowman	22	Newcastle	AB
John Brown	31	Newcastle	OS
Charles Chisholm	30	Newcastle	OS
John Cook	21	Newcastle	OS
Joseph Cook	31	Newcastle	OS
James Crawford	28	Durham	Quarter Gunner
John Dobson	29	Longhorsley	Quarter Gunner
David Donaldson	22	Newcastle	OS
John Dryden	47	Newcastle	Quarter Gunner
Richard Fairclough	23	Sunderland	LM
William Gaskell	29	Newcastle	OS
James Gardner	25	Newcastle	OS
Luke Guthrie	24	Gateshead	AB
Thomas Hardy	40	Newcastle	Quarter Gunner
James Hull	23	Durham	AB
John Hunter	32	Sunderland	QM
John James	22	Sunderland	OS
John Johnstone	24	Stockton	Carpenter's Mate
William Kentish	22	Newcastle	OS
George Maddison	21	Newcastle	OS
Joseph Nixon	23	Newcastle	OS
George Ovington	30	Sunderland	Quarter Gunner
Joseph Parker	22	Newcastle	OS
William Quickly	41	Berwick	AB
Benjamin Reynolds	27	North Shields	AB
David Ridley	40	Corbridge	OS
Richard Reavley	28	Berwick	Quarter Gunner
Joseph Robinson	23	Newcastle	AB
Thomas Sansby	38	Durham	QM
Matthew Stewart	39	Hartley	YS
John Watson	30	Dunstan	OS
Joseph Watts	22	Newcastle	OS
Henry Weatherburn	27	Newcastle	OS

Source: Ayshford Complete Trafalgar Roll.

Revenge

Name	Age	Place	Position
William Atkinson	21	Whitby	Trumpeter, Royal Marines
John Vickers	21	Chester-le-Street	Private, Royal Marines
George Wilson	30	Newcastle	AB
Robert Thompson	33	Shields	BM
John Oburne	26	Whitby	AB
William Nicholson	26	Scarborough	AB
William Carlisle	45	Berwick	AB
William West	23	Sunderland	AB
John Knagg	21	Ripon	OS
Matthew Davidson	32	Alnwick	LM
Robert Smith	38	Shields	AB
John Sheldon	28	North Shields	YS
Thomas Burnett	26	Sunderland	AB
Thomas Malterson	21	Sunderland	AB
Robert Rumford	34	Whitby	YS
William Robson	50	Newcastle	AB
Robert Reavley	30	Newcastle	AB
Thomas Burn	22	Whitby	OS
Robert Forrest	20	Shields	AB
Thomas Atkinson	35	Marske	LM
William Armour	20	Northumberland	AB
William Banks	42	Damsdale, N. Yorks	Carpenter's Crew
Jonathan Dawson	20	Shields	AB
Edward Robson	21	Shields	AB
Francis Routledge	25	Newcastle	LM
John Swinnibanks	24	Whitby	AB
Matthew Corney	21	Whitby	Mid
Thomas Jones	22	Sunderland	AB
Thomas Marshall	31	Shields	YS
Constantine R. Moorsom	13	Stokesley	Vol. 1st Class

Source: NA ADM 36/16546

Royal Sovereign

Name	Age	Place	Position
James Graydon	21	East Rainton, Durham	Quarter Gunner
Edward Gutterson	31	Newcastle	AB
John Eldrith	35	Stockton	AB
Joseph Ingram	31	Sunderland	Gunner's Mate
John Nisbett	28	Sunderland	Carpenter
George Jeffries	36	Berwick	Carpenter's Mate
Thomas Rutherford	28	Newcastle	AB
James Ryder	30	Richmond	Sailmaker's Mate
William Short	25	Sunderland	Quarter Gunner
George Castle	16	Durham	Mid
John Thompson	32	Stockton	AB
Grenville Thompson	18	Newcastle	Mid
John Westmorland	46	Lemington	LM
Robert Scott	25	Felton, Nthmbld.	Private, Royal Marines
William Willcox	24	Sunderland	AB

Source: NA ADM 36/15754

Victory

Name	Age	Place	Position
Thomas Atkinson	37	Richmond	MM
David Blake	22	Newcastle	AB
Lancelot Brown	47	Berwick	YPR
Robert Bookless	29	Tweedmouth	Coxswain
William Browis	20	North Shields	OS
Henry Butcher	26	Shields	AB
William Castle	29	Newcastle	BM
Robert Cloughton	34	Seaham	Private, Royal Marines
Nathaniel Cole	22	Sunderland	AB
George Colstone	23	Newcastle	Private, Royal Marines
George Darby	23	Newcastle	OS
Robert Darby	25	Darlington	AB
Robert Davidson	25	Sunderland	YS
Christopher Dixon	29	South Shields	QM
Isaac Dobson	27	Whitby	Cutter's Crew
George Fenwick	34	Newcastle	Gunner's Mate
William Forbes	44	North Shields	AB
Thomas Haggerty	22	Newcastle	AB
John Hunter	23	Newcastle	AB
William Hall	21	Newcastle	AB
George Ireland	53	North Shields	AB
Thomas Jarvis	43	Whitby	AB
John King	56	Sunderland	QM
Jonathan Marshall	46	Newcastle	QM
David Miffin	29	Newcastle	AB
William Morton	40	Fleetham, Nthmbld.	AB
William Patterson	24	Newcastle	AB
Alexander Penny	38	Northumberland	AB
Thomas Piercy	27	Scarborough	AB
Henry Searchwell	23	Newcastle	AB
Thomas Sedgewick	41	Sunderland	Quarter Gunner
William Spencer	28	Newcastle	YPR
William Smith	32	South Shields	AB
Benjamin Stevenson	24	Berwick	QM
George Stephenson	37	Whitby	AB
Robert Thompson	22	Shields	OS
William Thompson	24	North Shields	AB
Thomas Wood	42	Washington	AB

Source: www.cjbooks.demon.co.uk/eng.htm

Appendix Two

Trafalgar Casualties

Name	Age	Place	Position	Ship	Circumstances
James Scott	21	S. Shields	AB	Africa	Dow 5/12/05
John Kipling	29	Barn. Castle	BM	Africa	Wounded
William Barnes	26	Nthmbld.	AB	Belleisle	Wounded
John Harrison	24	Scarborough	AB	Belleisle	Wounded
John Todd	26	Sunderland	AB	Bellerophon	Kia 21/10/05
Michael Todd	26	Sunderland	YS	Bellerophon	Wounded
John Burton	26	Berwick	OS	Bellerophon	Wounded
Jonathan Eddison	21	Berwick	AB	Bellerophon	Wounded
Thomas Taylor	32	Berwick	AB	Bellerophon	Wounded
John Todd	26	S. Shields	AB	Britannia	Wounded
Robert Bell	34	Newcastle	RM	Britannia	Wounded
Wm. Anderson	20	Longbenton	AB	Colossus	Dow 23/10/05
Jacob Cairns	29	Newcastle	AB	Colossus	Dow 4/11/05
Sam. Somerville	20	Durham	AB	Colossus	Kia 21/10/05
George Trewhitt	21	Shields	AB	Colossus	Kia 21/10/05
Luke Anderson	35	Newcastle	MM	Colossus	Wounded
John Brown	22	Swalwell	OS	Colossus	Wounded
John Featherstone	33	Whitby	QM	Colossus	Wounded
Thomas Howey	31	N. Shields	AB	Colossus	Wounded
Rawdon Maclean	21	Berwick	MID	Colossus	Wounded

continued

Trafalgar Casualties

Name	Age	Place	Position	Ship	Circumstances
Matt. Winship	27	Newcastle	OS	Colossus	Wounded
Jacob Venus	22	N. Shields	AB	Colossus	Wounded
Hardin Hall	47	Sunderland	QM	Colossus	Wounded
John Bells	26	Durham	LM	Colossus	Wounded
John Hunter	23	Newcastle	AB	Defence	Wounded
James Kirk	23	Berwick	AB	Defence	Wounded
Thomas Manuel	27	Newcastle	AB	Defence	Wounded
Robert Ridley	45	Chester-le-Street	BM	Defence	Wounded
John Whittle	31	Newcastle	AB	Defence	Wounded
Stephen Bailey	22	Whitby	AB	Defiance	Wounded
John Stewart	36	N. Shields	AB	Defiance	Wounded
Josh Surtees	34	Newcastle	OS	Defiance	Wounded
David Arthur	47	Shields	AB	Dreadnought	Wounded
Wm. Danby	29	Whitby	AB	Dreadnought	Wounded
Henry Potts	22	S. Shields	AB	Dreadnought	Wounded
Thomas Walker	37	Berwick	BM	Leviathan	Wounded
Thomas Main	40	Stockton	QMM	Leviathan	Dow 15/11/05
Edward Lowe	28	Newcastle	AB	Leviathan	Wounded

continued

Trafalgar Casualties

Name	Age	Place	Position	Ship	Circumstances
James Thompson	35	Jarrow	AB	Leviathan	Wounded
Henry Wade	23	Nthmbld.	LM	Mars	Dow 02/06
William Graham	30	Newcastle	LM	Mars	Wounded
Wm. Andrews	22	Whitby	AB	Minotaur	Wounded
Phillip Eden	43	Hexham	OS	Minotaur	Wounded
Wm. West	23	Sunderland	AB	Revenge	Kia 21/10/05
George Wilson	30	Newcastle	AB	Revenge	Wounded
James Oburne	26	Whitby	AB	Revenge	Wounded
Wm.Nicholson	26	Scarborough	AB	Revenge	Wounded
Thomas Rutherford	28	Newcastle	AB	Royal Sovereign	Wounded
Grenville Thompson	16	Newcastle	MID	Royal Sovereign	Wounded
John Smith	23	Newcastle	AB	Swiftsure	Drowned On Redoubtable
Richard Hugh	23	Stockton	LM	Temeraire	Kia 21/10/05
Thomas Cole	25	Sunderland	OS	Temeraire	Dow 02/06
John Duncan	51	S. Shields	AB	Temeraire	Dow 01/06
Thomas Glendinning	51	Newcastle	YS	Temeraire	Wounded
Wm. Gordon	37	Newcastle	AB	Temeraire	Wounded
John Nicholson	21	Whitby	OS	Temeraire	Wounded

continued

Trafalgar Casualties

Name	Age	Place	Position	Ship	Circumstances
Wm. Featherston-ehaugh	49	Sunderland	QM	Temeraire	Drowned on Fougeaux
Alex. Galloway	14	Guisborough	MID	Thunderer	Wounded
James Woods	36	N. Shields	YS	Thunderer	Wounded
Robert Mills	23	Scarborough	AB	Tonnant	Wounded
Robert Davison	25	Sunderland	AB	Victory	Kia 21/10/05
James King	56	Sunderland	AB	Victory	Kia 21/10/05
Wm. Thompson	24	N. Shields	AB	Victory	Kia 21/10/05
David Blake	22	Newcastle	AB	Victory	Wounded
Lancelot Brown	47	Tweedmouth	YPR	Victory	Wounded
Wm. Castle	29	Newcastle	AB	Victory	Wounded
Thomas Haggerty	22	Newcastle	AB	Victory	Wounded
Wm. Hall	21	Newcastle	AB	Victory	Wounded
Isaac Dobson	27	Whitby	CARP CREW	Victory	Wounded
George Colston	23	Newcastle	RM	Victory	Wounded
George Darby	23	Newcastle	OS	Victory	Wounded

Abbreviations: KIA Killed in action, DOW Died of wounds

Appendix Three

Seamen Awarded the Trafalgar Medal

Name	Age	Position	Place	Ship
Alexander Dryborough	22	AB	Newcastle	AGAMEMNON
Thomas Robinson	24	AB	Sunderland	AGAMEMNON
Henry Purvis	26	OS	Berwick	AJAX
Robert Collinson	30	QM	Sunderland	BELLEISLE
Thomas Goodrich	26	Carpenter's Mate	Durham	COLOSSUS
William Gardner	25	OS	Blaydon	COLOSSUS
Thomas Willoughby	33	QM	Newcastle	CONQUEROR
William Dorman	29	Q. Gunner	Newcastle	DEFIANCE
Henry Potts	22	AB	South Shields	DREADNOUGHT
Joseph Bell	23	AB	Newcastle	EURYALUS
John Wm. Trotter	37	Master	Gateshead	LEVIATHAN
John Yellaly	22	LM	Newcastle	LEVIATHAN
James Thompson	35	AB	Jarrow	LEVIATHAN
William Andrews	22	AB	Whitby	MINOTAUR
Robert Newton	25	AB	Newcastle	NEPTUNE
George Maddison	21	OS	Newcastle	PRINCE
John Watson	30	OS	Dunstan	PRINCE
John Nisbett	28	Carpenter	Sunderland	ROYAL SOVEREIGN
Jonathan Pricely	24	AB	Sunderland	SIRIUS
Edward Davidson	25	LM	North Shields	SWIFTSURE
Roger Liddle	26	AB	Sunderland	SWIFTSURE
Alexander Galloway	14	Mid	Guisborough	THUNDERER
John Walker	23	AB	Sunderland	TONNANT
William Hall	21	AB	Newcastle	VICTORY

Note: The ages given are for 1805.

The Naval General Service Medal with Trafalgar Clasp was issued in 1848 and could only be claimed by former seamen who were alive at the time or by their relatives if the man died after June 1847. Applications for the medal closed in 1851. Less than ten per cent of those who fought at Trafalgar actually claimed the medal.

Source: Ayshford Complete Trafalgar Roll.

Select Bibliography

The maritime heritage of North East England is remarkable for its quality and diversity but remains under-researched by academic historians and under-appreciated by the public at large. The Year of the Sea, 2005, offers an exciting opportunity to raise the profile of this important aspect of regional history and, hopefully, stimulate new research. The following select bibliography offers a few suggestions for further reading for those who might wish to pursue their interest in the subjects raised within the book.

Adams, M. *Admiral Collingwood: Nelson's Own Hero.* Weidenfield and Nicholson (2005).

Adams, M. *Admiral Collingwood, Northumberland's Heart of Oak.* Tyne Bridge Publishing (2005).

Barrow, T. *The Whaling Trade of North East England 1750-1850.* University of Sunderland Press (2001).

Barrow, T. *Press Gangs and Privateers: Aspects of the Maritime History of North East England 1760-1815.* The Bewick Press (1993).

Clayton, T & Craig, P. *Trafalgar: the men, the battle, the storm.* Hodder and Stoughton (2004).

Coleman, T. *Nelson. The Man and the Legend.* Bloomsbury Publishing (2001).

Cordingly, D. *Billy Ruffian: The Bellerophon and the Downfall of Napoleon.* Bloomsbury Publishing (2004).

Deane, A. *Nelson's Favourite, H.M.S. Agamemnon at War, 1781-1809.* Naval Institute Press (1996).

Duffy, M. & Morriss, R. *The Glorious First of June: a naval battle and its aftermath.* Exeter University Press (2001).

Duggan, J. *The Great Mutiny.* Andre Deutsch (1966).

Jackson, H.W. *A County Durham Man at Trafalgar: Cumby of the Bellerophon.* Durham County Local History Society (1998).

Lavery, B. *Nelson's Navy: The Ships, Men and Organisation, 1793-1815.* Conway Maritime Press (1989).

Lavery, B. *Nelson's Fleet at Trafalgar.* National Maritime Museum (2004).

Lewis, M. *A Social History of the Navy, 1793-1815.* Allen & Unwin (1960).

Manwaring, G. E. & Dobree, B. *Mutiny: The Floating Republic.* The Cresset Library (1987).

Northcote-Parkinson, C. *Britannia Rules.* Alan Sutton Publishing (1994).

Orde, D. *Nelson's Mediterranean Command.* The Pentland Press (1997).

Osler, A. & Barrow, A. *Tall Ships: Two Rivers.* Keepdate (1993).

Richardson, W. *A Mariner of England.* Conway Maritime Press (1970).

Rodger, N. A. M. *The Wooden World: an Anatomy of the Georgian Navy.* Collins (1986).

Warner, O. *Life and Letters of Vice-Admiral Lord Collingwood.* Oxford University Press (1969).

Index

Publications

The Whaling Trade of North-East England 1750-1850
by Tony Barrow   ISBN 1 873757 83 2   Pages: 192   **Price: £14.95**
Plus postage and packing on single copies - £1.50

North East England was one of the most important centres of British whaling enterprise. From Berwick in the north to Whitby in the south, stoutly built whaling ships sailed annually to the Arctic grounds in search of the Greenland whale. The Whaling Trade of North-East England 1750-1850, is the first comprehensive, academic account of this fascinating aspect of the maritime heritage of the region.

Britain and the Baltic Studies in Commercial, Political and Cultural Relations 1500-2000 Edited by Tony Barrow and Patrick Salmon
ISBN 1873757 49 2   Pages: 384   **Price: £17.95**
Plus postage and packing on single copies - £2.50

Political, commercial and cultural connections between Britain and the Baltic are amongst the oldest and most enduring in the historical record. And yet, paradoxically, they are also amongst the least known and poorly understood. The essays contained within this volume demonstrate that scholarly study of Britain's historical relationship with the countries of Scandinavia and the Baltic region is both varied and dynamic.

Merchants and Gentry in North-East England 1650-1830
The Carrs and the Ellisons by A W Purdue
ISBN 1 873757 08 5   Pages: 304   ~~RRP £16.95~~ **Now £12.95**
Plus postage and packing on single copies - £2.50

This book follows the progress of the Ellisons of Hebburn Hall and the Carrs of Dunston Hill from their mercantile success in the seventeenth century to their solid gentry and land-owning status in the nineteenth century. The aim of this book is to set the history of the Carrs and Ellisons against the development of the region on which they made such an influence.

Sir Tom Cowie A True Entrepreneur – A Biography
by Denise Robertson – Foreword by Wilbur Smith
Hardback – ISBN 1 873757 30 1   Pages: 240   **Price: £16.99**
Paperback – ISBN 1 873757 84 0   Pages: 240   **Price: £8.99**
Plus postage and packing on single copies - £2.50

This is the storey of a young man from Sunderland who was discharged from the RAF in 1946 with a gratuity and went on to build one of the fastest-growing companies in the United Kingdom. The story moves from the small backyard where Tom Cowie's motor-cycle business started, through his days as manager and director of a successful lease-hire car company, to his accolades for political and other services.

Tom Hadaway The Prison Plays
Including Long Shadows co-written with Pauline Hadaway, Edited and with an introduction by Val McLane
ISBN 1 873757 10 7   Pages: 280   **Price: £12.95**
Plus postage and packing on single copies - £1.50

Tom Hadaway is one of North East England's leading playwrights. He has written more than twenty plays, films and television scripts, including *The Filleting Machine, God Bless Thee Jackie Maddison, Seafarers* and *The Long Line*, all performed by The Live Theatre in Newcastle. The Prison Plays is a collection of two full-length and two short plays written after his term as writer in residence at Durham and Frankland prisons in 1986.

A Concentration of Moral Force – The Temperance Movement in Sunderland, 1830 to 1853 by Allan Harty
ISBN 1 873757 93 X   Pages: 64   **Price: £7.95**
Plus postage and packing on single copies - £1.00

This study examines the evolution of the Temperance cause in Sunderland from its inception until the demand for parliamentary intervention heralded a new phase in the town's crusade against intemperance. Set against the prevailing culture of drink, the author discusses the conflict within the temperance movement as its objectives changed from 'moral suasion' to 'legislative suppression'.

Art & the Spiritual *Edited by Bill Hall and David Jasper*
ISBN 1 873757 78 6   Pages: 104   **Price: £14.95**
Plus postage and packing on single copies - £1.00

A collection of essays and responses; this book is challenging without retreating into the arcane world of academic debate and discussion. Written by artists, each essay is given a response by a professional theologian. .

The Millennium History of North East England
by David Simpson   ISBN 09536984 3 2   Pages: 336
Full Colour   Hardback   ~~RRP £24.99~~   **Now £7.50**
Plus postage and packing on single copies - £2.50

North East England has a strong sense of identity that sets it apart from other areas of England. This unique, beautifully illustrated hardback book explores the events, people and places that have shaped the region's history over the last two thousand years.

Northern Roots: Who we are, Where we come from, Why we speak the way we do *by David Simpson*
ISBN 1 901888 35 5   Pages: 160   **Price: £7.95**
Plus postage and packing on single copies - £1.50

Northerners speak with distinct local dialects and have their very own sense of history. But who are these Northerners and where did they come from? What clues exist in history to the ancient and more recent origins of Northerners and their speech?

North East England: places, history, people and legends
by David Simpson ISBN 1 901888 37 1   Pages: 224   **Price: £8.95**
Plus postage and packing on single copies - £1.50

North East England is a distinct region, with a unique culture and history. It is England's most northerly region and stretches from the Tees Valley and Cleveland Hills on the fringe of Yorkshire, one hundred miles north, to Berwick and the border with Scotland. This book is essentially about places and the part such places have played in the region's history.

The Official History of Sunderland AFC 1879-2000
Edited by John Hudson and Paul Callaghan
Hardback ISBN 09536984 1 6   Pages: 336   Full Colour
~~RRP £24.99~~ **Now £7.50**
Boxed ISBN 09536984 2 4   Pages: 336   Full Colour
~~RRP £39.99~~ **Now £10.00** *Plus p&p on single copies - £2.50*

Every season since the club's formation in 1879 is examined in detail - a saga that covers six League Championships, two FA Cup wins and seven promotions, with equal attention to the disappointing near misses, and the crushing blows of relegation. This book with over 400 illustrations is the most comprehensive account of the club's 120 year history.

Old Wives' Tales: remedies pills and potions *by Carol Cooke,*
Illustrations by Sheila Graber
ISBN 1 901888 32 0   Pages: 80   **Price: £4.95**
Plus postage and packing on single copies - £1.00

There's nothing Northern folks like better than getting together for an evening's entertainment. And what better entertainment is there than a walk down memory lane, discussing ancient ailments and alarming cures?

Old Wives' Tales: sheep's-head broth, sausages and sago
by Carol Cooke – Illustrations by Sheila Graber
ISBN 1 901888 38 X   Pages: 96   **Price: £4.95**
Plus postage and packing on single copies - £1.00

Carol Cooke's book weighs up northern cookery, and deals with the following burning, or simmering questions: How many parts of an animal can you reasonably eat? What is bible tripe and do you have to be holy to enjoy it?

To order any of the above publications you can either Fax, Telephone or contact: Business Education Publishers Limited, The Teleport, Doxford International, Sunderland, SR3 3XD, **Tel:** +44(0) 191 5252410, **Fax:** +44(0) 191 5201815, **email:** info@bepl.com